IMAGES OF ENGLAND

Walsall
remembered

from Jenny christmas 2010

IMAGES OF ENGLAND

Walsall
remembered

Jack Haddock & Ruth Vyse

The History Press

Frontispiece: Royal Scot locomotive No. 46115, *c.* 1963. The locomotive is shown leaving Walsall station to take the north-bound Pines Express to Manchester. The express was diverted via Walsall station for the summer service only.

First published in 2004 by Tempus Publishing

Reprinted in 2009 by
The History Press
The Mill, Brimscombe Port,
Stroud, Gloucestershire, GL5 2QG
www.thehistorypress.co.uk

British Library Cataloguing in Publication Data.
A catalogue record for this book is available from the British Library.

ISBN 978 0 7524 3294 6

Typesetting and origination by Tempus Publishing
Printed in Great Britain.

Contents

Acknowledgements

The authors would like to thank Joyce Hammond and staff past and present of Walsall Local History Centre for their support and encouragement. Thanks are due to the *Walsall Observer* and Simmons Aerofilms for permission to reproduce news cuttings and photographs. The authors would also like to thank the others who contributed to the book by sharing the memories and photographs recorded here. In addition, thanks are due to Christopher Murrells for scanning and preparing the text and to David Fink.

Introduction

The text of this book and many of the photographs are the work of Jack Haddock. The photographs were chosen by and the captions written by Ruth Vyse, manager of Walsall Local History Centre. Jack Haddock was born in 1927. In 1928 his family moved into their new council house in Webster Road and Jack has lived there ever since. As the book recounts, he has had a lifelong interest in transport of all kinds: roads, canals and railways. He began work at fourteen at the Walsall Corporation bus depot on Bloxwich Road, Birchills, and stayed there for four years. At eighteen he served in the Royal Air Force and after that was employed in the metal trade. Jack has been a keen photographer all his life. He recognised the importance of recording the local landscape, particularly where it was about to change from the 1950s onwards. He has preserved therefore an often unique record of a world which has changed dramatically in the last fifty years. The Jack Haddock collection is particularly rich in transport photographs but covers other areas as well. Jack recognised not only the importance of the visual record but of recorded memory too. Much of the material in this book, as well as recording Jack's own memories, also records the memories of others. These range from Fred Parker recalling the family timber yard and animals passing through Leamore to railwaymen recalling the shift system at the parcels office and the journeys of hop pickers to Herefordshire and Shropshire. Not only did Jack write down these memories, he also tape recorded interviewees to preserve their memories in their own words. Both photographs and tape recordings form an invaluable part of the collections at Walsall Local History Centre. I am happy to report that Jack is still adding to them, for example by compiling a photographic record of the building of Walsall's new art gallery. All of these activities are made easier because Jack still cycles daily as he did in his school days. We hope that he will continue to travel and record for many years to come.

   The era which this book chronicles covers much of the twentieth century. It is particularly rich, however, in material for the period 1920-1945. The book provides a fascinating glimpse of how much ordinary life has changed and how rapidly during this period. A few examples will suffice. The account of the injured Jack Smith's journey to hospital on a horse-drawn cart covered by a canvas sheet on a cold winter's night reminds us of how medical treatment and transport has changed. The section on the difference the coming of the wireless made to people's lives reminds us how in the twentieth century we moved from the era of the newspaper and the telegraph through the wireless to the television, the computer and the mobile phone. Both Mrs Ball's account of life in Canal Street and the description of the variety of services provided by the railway between the wars remind us of an age when most people did not have cars and goods were transported by railway and canal, not road. The account of summer holidays in North Walsall reminds us of an age when the steam train reigned supreme and provided a perennial source of fascination to children.

Walsall developed as a market town in the medieval and early modern period. Industry developed in the eighteenth and nineteenth centuries, prompted by the local supplies of coal, limestone and ironstone and by the building of canals and railways. Saddlers' ironmongery was a medieval industry and from this the leather trade developed in the nineteenth century. With increased prosperity went industrial and residential development. The photographs in the text show Walsall as it was in the 1920s through to the 1960s. Some of them reflect the changing scene, e.g. the development of transport, of cinemas and new housing. Others show the town as it had developed from the sixteenth century onwards before the changes in the 1960s.

The medieval town centred around St Matthew's church at the top of the High Street. From there the centre moved down to The Bridge where it has stayed. At one time trams and buses terminated on The Bridge itself before the first bus station was built in the 1930s. At that time the George Hotel dominated the scene. Going on down Park Street the station façade built in the 1920s was a prominent feature, as was Her Majesty's Theatre at Town End, replicated now in the current Woolworths building. Rows of tightly packed houses clustered round Wisemore at the bottom of Stafford Street. Stafford Street itself was developed throughout the nineteenth century as ribbon development moved further and further out. By 1906 the Essex Street estate had been built to be followed in the late 1920s by Webster Road and its companion streets. The sand pit at the end of the street stayed as open ground thanks to the local business man who left it to the town. Local industry was part of the scene in Green Lane, the canal at Pratt's Bridge, the railway at Ryecroft and the small businesses in Portland Street and the neighbouring area. In the 1920s and 1930s it was still possible to walk across fields from Leamore to Birchills. All of this was the background to the account of life given here.

The photographs which illustrate the text are taken from the Jack Haddock collection, including a number taken by Jack himself, and the other photographic collections held by the Local History Centre. They complement the text itself or provide a visual record of Walsall at the period recounted in the text or later before major changes were made to the town landscape.

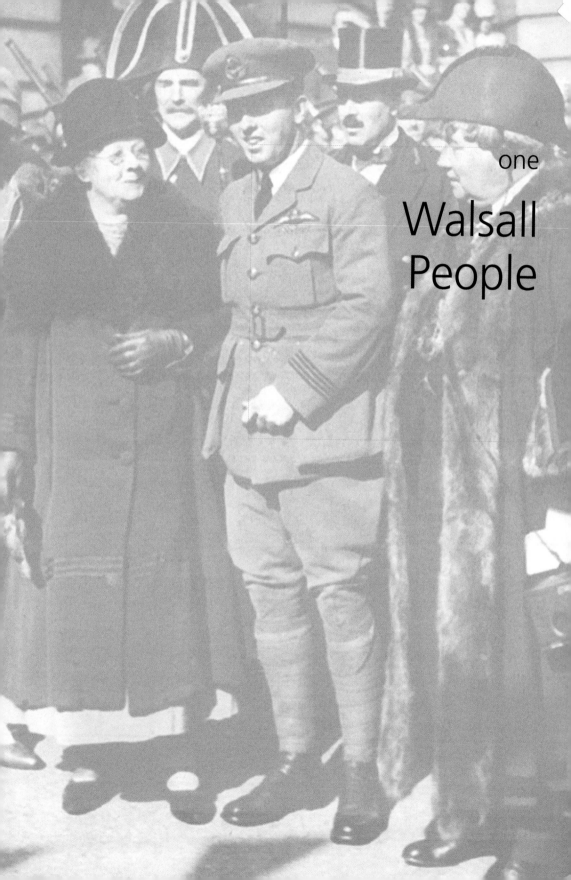

one

Walsall
People

Jack Smith

Jack Smith was born at 13 Marlow Street in 1892. His father was a miner and reared a family of two sons and one daughter. Life was very hard and a constant battle was waged to attain a decent standard of living. Jack attended John Street School and was a very good pupil. He was never involved in trouble nor absent from school. He was always fond of reading the Bible and did so until the end of his life. Jack and his family were never in any trouble or conflict with society or the law despite the constant struggle to make ends meet. Trips to the seaside or theatre were unknown and the cheapest form of leisure was taking long walks at the appropriate time of the year. A walk to Birmingham and back to look around the shops was a day's outing, but to buy anything was out of the question. Refreshment was in the form of taking apples and oranges and obtaining drinking water from public conveniences. For home entertainment the Smith family possessed a small organ that Jack learned to play when young. He spent many hours playing his favourite hymns.

In 1906 Jack started work down the pit. His first pit was the Leighswood Colliery at Aldridge. He worked long hours for only about £1 a week. At first Jack had to walk to work, but after some time he managed to save enough money to purchase a reliable cycle. Jack remembers that most of the local miners either walked or cycled to Aldridge. They did this firstly to save money and secondly because if a miner could afford the rail fare he was not welcome in a railway carriage because of his filthy clothing and would be treated like scum by other passengers. The working conditions at Leighswood Colliery were grim and in 1910 Jack decided to try his luck elsewhere. He found a job at Holly Bank Colliery and for a time thought he was on to a good thing, with a slight rise in pay and less dusty conditions. However, fate took a hand one day in 1913 when Jack had the misfortune to be struck by a rake of loaded coal tubs that had run away. His injuries consisted of a broken hip, a broken leg and rib fractures. This accident happened during mid-winter on a night shift and before the days of an organised ambulance service.

The Sixty Steps footbridge, about 1955-1964. This was a narrow footbridge at the bottom of Cartbridge Lane between Rushall and Ryecroft. There was a row of steps both sides and a series of planks to walk across with guard rails on either side with very ornate iron work. The bridge was demolished in the early 1970s. It was here that Jack Smith stood to await the swallows each year.

Unveiling of memorial cross at Ryecroft Cemetery, 1925. The cemetery in Coalpool Lane was opened in 1894. The cross was unveiled by the then mayor, D.E. Parry. It commemorates soldiers and sailors who died in the First World War and are buried in the cemetery.

a temporary ambulance. A canvas sheet was erected over the cart and the floor was strewn with straw and sacks for Jack to lie on to give as much comfort as possible from the roads (which consisted at that time of only dirt tracks). The nearest hospital to Holly Bank Colliery was New Cross, Wolverhampton. After a time that seemed like an eternity to Jack, a horse and driver were provided and the trek to hospital started. It was a clear moonlit night as Jack lay suffering. The cartwheels lurched from rut to rut, each movement giving much distress because of his painful injuries. To make matters worse, Jack began to feel the frost forming on his body, and, by the time they reached the hospital, he was unconscious. He spent a month in hospital and after three months' convalescence the doctors informed Jack that he would have a stiff leg for the rest of his life and would never be free from a certain amount of pain around his left hipbone. Before Jack returned to work he was asked to attend an enquiry with the colliery management and was granted compensation of £100, a considerable sum in 1913.

During his convalescence Jack sought work elsewhere, only to find nothing available. Only pit work was offered, which Jack took reluctantly for financial security. With the advent of the First World War anyone with mining experience had to work in the pits. Jack could not be called up for army service owing to his disability. He could not face work again at Holly Bank Colliery and worked at the Norton and Cannock Colliery near Great Wyrley, often on twelve-hour shifts. During mid-winter Jack never saw daylight or the sun for many weeks. If there was a fall of heavy snow he got to Bloxwich by tram then walked through the drifts along the lanes. The miners gradually made trenches through the deep snow. This reminded Jack of soldiers in France marching in columns, as groups of miners plodded their way to and from their grim existence below ground.

During the Depression Jack left the Norton and Cannock Colliery to work at Mid Cannock, West Cannock and Harrison's Collieries. He spent the last twenty-one years of his pit life at Harrison's No. 3 Colliery, retiring in 1956 after fifty years below ground. Jack had no retirement present, just a handshake from the manager and a farewell from

The Ditch, Ablewell Street, 1938. Two roads led up from Ablewell Street to St Matthew's church by the later seventeenth century, one was the Ditch. As seen here, it was one of the streets of densely packed housing which covered the hill around St Matthew's church. Much of the housing was cleared in the 1930s and the occupants moved to Goscote and Harden.

Stafford Street, 1974. Dennis Kimpton's newsagents shop is shown in the background. There were buildings along the southern end of Stafford Street by the early nineteenth century and development as far as the canal by its end. However by 1971 shops in Stafford Street had decayed because of competition from town centre shops and uncertainty about the projected ring road.

the lads as he picked up his last pay packet. He still suffered pain from his leg and hip and had thoughts of just sitting about and resting for the rest of his life. However, he decided to spend as much time as possible walking around the Walsall district to keep active. His favourite walks were along the local canals and in the parks, during good weather. During early spring I would always find Jack near the Sixty Steps footbridge, over the old South Staffordshire railway line, patiently awaiting the arrival of the swallows from Africa. The first one he saw gave him great pleasure to know that summer was imminent and I was duly informed. Just watching nature and breathing fresh air was to Jack a tonic after his many years within the bowels of the earth. Every Sunday evening, Jack would attend one of Walsall's local churches alone to enjoy the service. Nevertheless he always stressed his disappointment at the congregation's lack of friendliness. However, Jack was not bitter with life and just went about his way without any animosity or ill feeling toward anyone.

In 1959, Jack's old house in Marlow Street was demolished and he went to live at 50 Proffitt Street with his sister as the rest of the family had passed away. She was taken ill and Jack cared for her until she passed away in 1961. The house was cold and damp in winter and Jack was finding life difficult, especially as his pit injuries gave him more pain as he grew older. In 1967 the council Social Services department found Jack a pensioner's bungalow at Mill Place. Most of his furniture was left at 50 Proffitt Street; just his bed, sideboard, table and a few chairs were all he required for his basic needs, but room was found for his beloved organ, which he still played occasionally. By 1969 Jack could hardly walk and was confined to his bungalow, with a home help visiting him twice a week. In 1973, Jack was found dead, alone, and had not been missed. Thus ended a life of hardship and pain. To this day, I always remember Jack, especially when I see a swallow.

Bert Wood

Bert Wood passed away in 1987 aged eighty-two. All his life was spent in the Ryecroft district of Walsall. His father was a miner who had the misfortune to be killed in a roof fall at Walsall Wood Colliery. Employment was uncertain in Ryecroft between the two world wars. Bert's mother did receive compensation for this father's death, a sum of approximately £100. This was a small fortune in those days and his mother was very conservative with this income. She had Bert's brother and sister to keep also. Bert Wood left school at fourteen and was employed in various local foundries, moving from one to another at the whim of the 'slave trade' bosses of that era. Bert and his younger brother, Harry, managed to sustain their family until the advent of the Second World War. Being just over military age, Bert Wood was drafted into the local and national Civil Defence. He saw many of the air raids on Coventry, Birmingham, London and the Isle of Wight and he witnessed many morbid sights during England's finest hour.

When hostilties ceased Bert found employment with Walsall Corporation's public works department. Despite his modes of employment, mainly as a labourer, he had acquired a brilliant mathematical brain, especially with respect to mental arithmetic. Bert Wood was, after the 1930s hardships, in the happy position of having a regular job plus some government gratuity for war work. Having surplus cash, Bert Wood's regular bookmaker was a Mr Billy Evans, residing in nearby Mill Street. On his frequent visits to this bookmaker, Bert would often confront Billy Evans when underpaid on certain winning bets. Billy Evans concluded that Bert was always right due to his mental arithmetic prowess. Thus he instructed his staff that whenever Bert appeared in the office he was to be given whatever amount he stated. It is a well-known fact that bookmakers on average took more profit than paying out winnings. Bert, by the approaching 1970s, must have lost many hundred of pounds on betting. One day in 1976, he happened to be passing the local West Midland Bank and wished good morning to Billy Evans departing down the bank's steps. 'Good morning Bert,' replied Billy Evans. 'Would you like a lift back to Ryecroft?' pointing to a rather new and expensive car parked adjacent to the bank. Bert Wood paused then deposited himself on the front passenger seat. 'I might as well have a ride in your new car, being as I have bought the bloody thing for you!' he said.

Syd Webster

As an infant pupil in Butts School, George Cooper became friends with a small freckle-faced lad called Syd Webster. Prior to the First World War, life in the Butts was concerned with family virtues and children like George Cooper and Syd Webster acquired a good primary education from the very firm and dedicated teachers of that era. They were nevertheless fair with the children and gave them encouragement to progress in life. One teacher advised them to go on long walks in the countryside to view and observe nature and wildlife. In those days, the countryside was close by. One day in the summer holidays George and young Webster along with others were engaged in a summer ramble to Barr Beacon and were returning from the direction of Park Lime Pits and Rushall Hall. At this point there happened to break out a severe thunderstorm and torrential rain.

The gang of lads ran for shelter under a small cattle bridge under the Midland Railway line from Walsall to Sutton. The storm became ferocious, with forked lightning and loud thunder. As the storm raged, these young lads were on the verge of panic. Young Webster burst into tears and began to pray to God to stop the storm. Very shortly the storm abated and the Butts' gang returned home. As these Butts' children grew up they lost contact with each other. Webster became a good scholar and many years later George Cooper learned that Syd Webster had become a Royal Air Force pilot. He and many other locals were thrilled when Flight-Lieutenant Webster, as he had become, won the 1927 Air Race flying a Supermarine SS seaplane to take the Schneider Trophy.

In the late 1920s George Cooper began to raise a family after a few years in the Royal Navy and eventually applied to rent one of the new council houses being built in the late 1920s and early 1930s. After some time he was allocated a house a No. 84 Webster Road, a street named in honour of his old school pal. When George Cooper related this story to me he remarked that Syd Webster had overcome his fears and anxiety to become the first airman to fly at 281.65mph, to hold the world's air-speed record and to become a Walsall citizen with a place in history.

Flight-Lieutenant Webster at Walsall Council House reception, 1927. The reception was held to honour Webster's victory in the Schneider Trophy international seaplane race at Venice when he flew faster than anyone had flown before and brought the trophy back to the United Kingdom. Webster is shown with his mother, the mayor and mayoress and the borough MP. Webster Road was named after the flight-lieutenant.

Flight-Lieutenant Webster in Walsall, 1927. The whole town turned out to welcome Webster on his return to Walsall after his victory. Following the presentations in Walsall Council House, there was a luncheon for 200 people. In the evening there was a torchlight procession and a firework display.

High Street near Old Square, 1960. This was before development in the 1960s. The development changed the view up the High Street by creating a new shopping precinct in the top half of Digbeth and the Old Square which went north from Digbeth to Freer Street.

Ernest Fisher

Ernest William Fisher was born in the Chuckery district of Walsall in 1905. He recalled vividly visiting a field near Springvale Farm on the Birmingham Road, very close to the demolished Malt Shovel public house, now the site of the Boundary Hotel. This was in 1913 and the event was probably the first visit of aeroplanes to Walsall. The occasion was an air race between two pioneer aviators, Mr gustav Hamel and Mr B.C. Hucks. It was a circular race around the Midlands, landing and taking off at a number of suitable fields. Ernest Fisher well remembered a vast crowd witnessing this precursor of the present-day flying era. To him it seemed that most of Walsall walked to Springvale Farm. Today, if a helicopter lands within the Borough of Walsall it hardly warrants a few glances!

Ernest Fisher grew up to lead a normal, fairly uneventful life, marrying with one son. He gave almost six years to the British Army during the Second World War, during which time he became well aware of the progress being made in aviation. After army service he worked until retirement age and eventually moved to a bungalow in Kent Close.

In 1988 his wife spotted an advert in the local newspaper advertising a special three-hour trip for senior citizens in British Airways' Concord. They applied and were invited to Heathrow Airport, London, for a flight over the Bay of Biscay. The trip included a special coach from Birmingham to Heathrow plus a first class meal on the flight.

When I saw Ernest Fisher afterwards he commented that he had lived during an age that had seen primitive aeroplanes through to those which flew beyond the speed of sound. He almost thought it was a dream. Ernest Fisher passed away in 1989.

Mrs Ball: Life in Canal Street and Birchills, 1914-1939

Mrs Ball was a native of Derby who came to Walsall at the outbreak of the First World War to seek employment on war work. She was successful in finding work at Kynocks

Munitions Factory at Aston, Birmingham. Although she worked long hours, the financial reward was substantial compared to pre-war days. After leaving school she had been lucky to be taken on as a chorus girl at a Derby theatre. She accompanied famous artists of the halcyon days of the music hall, such as Marie Studholm, Vesta Tilly, Florrie Ford and Nellie Wallace. She found lodgings in Walsall and met a local lad who worked at Lindops Foundry in Pleck. They got married shortly afterwards and found a house in Canal Street, situated to the rear of the large flour mill in Wolverhampton Street that was built in 1848.

Mrs Ball soon found out it was not a great place of comfort. They lived in a row of small houses with a communal washhouse and privies in a small yard to the rear. Facing the house was the murky, foul-smelling canal with three locks situated within a stone's throw of their front door. With approximately one hundred canal boats passing by from about 6.00 a.m. until 12.00 p.m., the problem of noise from the constant rattling of paddles from the nearby locks took some getting used to. It took her about twelve months of this cacophony to settle in. From the mill itself came the smell of flour, plus the rattling of chains descending from the top storey of the mill after hoisting bags from the wheat boats belonging to the Severn and Canal Carrying Company. The boat people were very happy, hard working, peaceful citizens despite being looked down upon by certain members of upper-class society. Boat people used to call on Mrs Ball or her neighbours for permission to use the community drinking water in the yard to fill their water cans. Friendships developed and often on late evenings, especially weekends, much time would be spent in the nearby public houses, the Elephant and Castle and the Engine Inn. After closing time the boat people made their way back to the canal to produce a melodeon and treat the residents of Canal Street to a most entertaining musical end to the day.

These Canal Street residents also had to put up with the noise of the mill machinery that operated for twenty-four hours a day. Another problem was the ever-present company of rats that thrived on the combination of flour and canal water. Not helping matters was the presence of a large foundry situated opposite the mill end of Canal Street. With the wind in the north, fumes and dust from this foundry made life unbearable and played havoc with the washing.

Living next door to Mrs Ball was one of Walsall's characters, a Mr Wood. With a head of hair that was snow white he acquired the nickname 'White Knob Wood'. He was affluent enough to own coal boats and horses and, with regular orders from local factories, was fortunate enough to be well off financially in the post-First World War years of depression. He used to go on the town on weekends in style, dressing like a toff and carrying gold sovereigns. Subsequently he mixed a lot with the town's muggers and con men, thus acquiring the habit of drinking heavily. Often he was robbed of his cash by his so-called friends when in an alcoholic stupor. This led to constant rows and arguments with his long-suffering wife. An episode occurred one Saturday dinnertime that is still remembered today by the old folk of Birchills. After a midday drinking session in the White Lion public house on the corner of Green Lane and Hospital Street, White Knob was boasting of his ability to climb a sixty-foot chimney stack situated opposite belonging to Thomas's Iron Works. With the beer flowing through his veins he ascended the steel ladder and climbed upwards. He was about halfway up the stack when his confidence suddenly deserted him. Panic prevailed and after a while White Knob was screaming out for his mother to rescue him. By this time a large crowd had gathered to view this stupid stunt, including children from miles around, as the news passed along the street's grapevine. The police arrived and called the fire brigade, who were trained to climb

Top: *Small factories at the rear of Lower Portland Street backing on to Rue Meadow or Bulls Field, 1959. F. Staples' store was a wallpaper, paint and decorating business. The area continued to house small firms until at least the 1960s. In 1961 these included a signwriter and commercial vehicle painter, a currier and leather dresser, a plant hire contractor and a leather goods manufacturer.*

Above: *Ryecroft Farm, early twentieth century. In the early eighteenth century the farm was part of the Rushall Hall estate. The corporation bought the farm in 1919 and laid it out as part of the site of a council estate. Part was also laid out as nineteen cottage holdings of one acre each for ex-servicemen.*

ladders like steeplejacks. One of their members climbed up behind him and coaxed White Knob down step by step. After an eternity White Knob was brought down to 'terra firma' to loud cheers from the vast crowd of onlookers. It was certainly a memorable occasion for those residents of Birchills who witnessed it.

This episode did not deter White Knob from his drinking habit, however. The residents of Canal Street were well acclimatised to the rows with his wife, but the incident with the chimney stack was not forgotten by the locals. His wife often tried to deter White Knob from setting out on his drinking habits and persuade him to stop at home – to no avail. At the bottom of the communal yard White Knob had a small plot of rented land which he used for rearing pigs, but the job of feeding and cleaning them fell to Mrs Wood. Sometime after acquiring the first pigs she made up her mind for a man who specialised in killing pigs to call one evening to do the necessary so that they could enjoy some fresh pork for a few meals and also sell some to neighbours. On the evening the pig man called, White Knob had left the house for a pub crawl after a thundering row with his wife. Her last words to him had been, 'I might as well be bloody dead as put up with this life with you for ever'. Mrs Wood retired to bed and, well past midnight, White Knob came home in his usual alcoholic stupor to stagger into the house via the scullery. After some effort he lit a candle to light his way to bed. It cast an eerie reflection on the shroud-covered pig, slaughtered earlier. His beer-sodden brain reacted to this spooky sight and his wife's parting words suddenly rang in his ears: 'I might as well be bloody dead'. White Knob panicked. He ran next door to Mrs Ball. She was soon roused by his frantic hammering on the front door and came downstairs to be confronted by the words, 'Mrs Ball please go and find a policeman at once. My old gel has hung herself in the scullery'. He collapsed on Mrs Ball's sofa crying as she hastily dressed and made off past the flour mill and down Wolverhampton Street to find the nearest foot patrol policeman. She found one who immediately responded to the situation, escorting Mrs Ball swiftly to the scene of the tragedy. The police constable told Mrs Ball to remain outside the scullery while he examined the hanging shroud. Meanwhile White Knob was on the living room sofa fast asleep. Ripping the shroud off the hanging carcass the police constable suddenly cried, 'It's a bloody pig not a human!' White Knob was then roused from his alcoholic slumber by the irate constable who had to decide whether to prosecute him for wasting police time. The constable decided not to do so after the offer of a leg of pork. The news of the funny episode was soon around the Birchills district and, along with the chimney stack performance, is still remembered to this very day.

The entrance to Canal Street, under the flour mill from Wolverhampton Street, was, at times, used for certain human requirements. It was very useful to shelter there during heavy rain along with courting couples in the dim, gloomy, gas-lit evenings. Small recesses into the mill were very useful for young lovers at night. During daytime the street bookmakers found the mill nook holes an ideal situation for their illegal practice. One evening a local lady from Wolverhampton Street knocked on Mrs Ball's door with a coin in her hand and asked to be shown into the living room to view the coin in the glare of the gaslight. She let out a scream and wailed, 'It's a penny, Mrs Ball, the lousy, rotten dog'. The lady, it transpired, was a member of the oldest profession in the world. Her fee for the immoral practice in those days was half a crown but this cad had taken advantage of the poor light and passed her one penny. 'I'll get even with him,' the lady said to Mrs Ball. 'You meet me at the corner of Pleck Road at one o'clock tomorrow dinnertime as the gentleman comes home to dinner from Walker Brothers' Factory.'

Mrs Ball kept the appointment to see the outcome of the previous night's bad bargain. The man duly arrived, eagerly anticipating a well-cooked meal by his faithful wife. The cheated lady began to walk alongside her previous night's customer who inquired, 'Where are you making for my lady?' She replied, 'I am coming home with you to tell your wife you cheated me out of two shillings five pence for my previous night's services'. Mrs Ball was highly amused at this lady's method of dealing with this selfish cheat of a man. The man's fear of his wife finding out his adulterous nature left him no option but to pay up and he swiftly walked home to dinner, leaving Mrs Ball and the lady of easy virtue highly amused.

Most of the residents of Canal Street rarely left the vicinity of the junction of Wolverhampton Street and Pleck Road. Most of the men worked in the many Pleck Road factories with wives content to stay at home looking after domestic affairs. The area was so industrialised that within a mile of Canal Street one could see in excess of one hundred chimney stacks all at most times belching smoke into the atmosphere. Local people had no need to shop away from the Pleck Road junction, for shops were available for all needs. One such establishment was Bradshaw's, a shoe shop. One evening in the 1920s it was subject to a fire that severely damaged the premises. The fire was promptly dealt with by the fire brigade. A lot of stock was saved but was soaked with water. Boots and shoes were scattered about the area and not surprisingly many passers by took a liking to the footwear bonanza. It was on a Saturday night that the fire broke out and when the public houses turned out the crowds gathered. It was during the night, after the fire brigade had returned to base, that certain deeds took place in the absence of the police foot patrol. It was very early on Sunday morning that Mr Bradshaw assessed the damage to find shoe losses on a large scale. The police were informed and took action by house-to-house searches nearby. The police were so successful that they brought a handcart to deliver the stolen shoes to Goodall Street police station with the culprits' names tied to them. A special court was set up to deal with the offenders, amongst whom was a Mr West. Mr West resided in the large corner house standing on the corner of Pleck Road and Wolverhampton Road adjacent to Rigby's, the well-known grocery shop. He was a man of considerable status by virtue of being the local area manager of the Mond Gas Company of Tipton who supplied gas for industrial purposes to the Pleck district of Walsall. A nameplate above his front door affirmed his position. It was most humiliating for Mr West who with lesser mortals was subsequently summoned and fined £5 for looting. Mrs Ball and friends, who were not involved in this, remember the event, and many of the culprits had to endure rude remarks and ragging for many months afterwards.

Mrs Ball always had good relations with the poor working-class community that lived in the vicinity of the flour mill and was always referred to as 'Derby'. She passed away in Gladstone House in 1979, living in the comfort of a warden-controlled old people's home, in contrast to the damp, air-polluted atmosphere of Canal Street.

Fred Parker

Fred was one of three brothers who owned a timber yard in Green Lane on the site subsequently occupied by the Tube Investments factory by Green Lane canal bridge. This was the third timber yard owned by the Parker family. The second timber yard was on the site of the South Staffordshire Glue Works, now the site of the South Staffordshire Water

Works offices. This timber yard was burned down in 1905. Fred's father built the first timber yard in the 1850s, which was situated near the Trooper public house in the Harden district.

Fred was born in a small cottage in Providence Lane, Leamore. His schooling took place at Leamore Board School opposite the Spread Eagle public house. Discipline was very strict at this school. The headmaster was a Mr Sam Porter and the teachers were Dickie Marshall, Fred Whatton, Ted Bayford, Alf Jennings, Bob Patterson and Lawrie Hilton. All the staff exercised their authority and often used the tawse for punishment. Only the basic subjects were taught, with English and mathematics periods predominating. Recreation was an hour for lunch and a ten-minute break both morning and afternoon. However the top class were allowed one hour's swimming at Walsall Baths each Friday afternoon. All children had to march from Leamore to Walsall and back. On the way back to school from Providence Lane, Fred remembers passing a large house standing back from the road on the site of what was the Rosum Cinema. It had a large garden with a number of fowl, ducks and geese who wandered on the main road, only moving when steam trams and later electric trams rattled by.

As a small lad Fred was carried around Leamore on his dad's back. A treat for Fred was to visit the steam trams at the Red Lion terminus. The drivers and conductors passed the time until departure to Walsall in the Red Lion. Fred's father often took him on the steam engine and when the men came out of the pub they had a short ride on the foot plate and Fred well remembers the filth and smell of coke fumes, together with falling cinders. The drivers were Billy Morris, Jack Cockayne, Tommy Boden and Sid Bradbury. Bill Morris was the good-living man of this quartet who throughout his life lived to a true Victorian code. Just before the steam trams gave way to electric traction they evidently became the worse for wear. Ascending Pratt's Bridge with a full load, Fred and his father often saw a tram stall for lack of steam. The procedure was to run backwards towards North Walsall to raise a fresh head of steam and take a long run at the hill. Fred's parents regarded the steam tram most unfavourably and soon travelled on electric trams on account of their cleanliness.

An occasional event for Leamore was the visit of a herd of goats. These often numbered over 200 or more with about four men in charge. Milk from the goats was sold to householders for two pence a pint, or goats could be sold to those who were affluent enough to afford an animal for their own needs. The travelling goat herds evidently covered vast distances, visiting almost every town and small communities like Leamore within the Midlands.

As a small lad Fred recalls the sight of Mr Pratt (junior) and a friend mounting their horses in full hunting attire in the yard of Pratt's Mill on the Bloxwich Road next to the canal. He used to run after them to Leamore Lane where they were joined by more horsemen to make their way to Bloxwich Hall to pick up dogs from the kennels situated at the rear of the hall. Fred then used to watch them assemble in their full glory and when they were ready they would head along Elmore Green and then along Broad Lane to join others at Squire Vernon's hall at Essington.

Young Fred was occasionally taken on a trip with local publicans and characters of doubtful repute. From his father's pub, the Railway Inn on Bloxwich Road, Leamore, they travelled by brake to a farm in the vicinity of Brewood. The reason for this isolation was to indulge in the sport of cock fighting, along with the gambling associated with it. On return to Leamore, everyone engaged in this so-called afternoon of sport retired to a local pub, more often than not the Black Horse in Leamore, to share out the winnings.

Demolition of Birchills Ironworks stack, Green Lane, c. 1930. The Walsall Glue Co. is shown in the background. The firm started as a glue and gelatine works, c. 1870. In 1872 it was bought by a group of local men and traded as Townsend & Co. Ltd. A new works was built in Green Lane on the Wyrley & Essington Canal. It appears to have closed between 1962 and 1971. This would have been familiar territory to Fred Parker.

Birchills Foundry canal arm, 1965. The three redundant canal boats in the picture, Rodney, Cambrian *and* Victory, *are a reminder of how much coal was carried by canal in the late nineteenth and early twentieth centuries. Birchills Foundry began operations in the 1850s. Sister Dora, Walsall's nursing pioneer, nursed workers at the foundry injured in an explosion in 1875. The foundry closed around 1925. It would have been familiar to Fred Parker when working at the family timber yard.*

By evening everyone staggered home in a high state of intoxication. Fred only made a few trips with this fraternity, because the whole business filled him with disgust. Cock fighting had been made illegal many years previously, but Fred knew it continued out of sight of the police for many years after.

Whilst Fred was living at the Railway Inn, his mother died in 1901. As a result Fred was soon taught the pub routine. The inn was open from 6.00 a.m. until midnight. Each year Fred's father took the pub's regulars on a horse and brake trip to Bridgnorth, starting out at 6.00 a.m. and on one occasion left Fred, at the age of ten, in charge of the pub. When it came to closing time the brake had not returned so Fred closed the pub and awaited their arrival, which turned out to be 6.00 a.m. – opening time for the next day. It transpired that the whole party was drunk on departure and after only a few miles one of the two horses had collapsed and died. The driver carried on with one horse at slow speed and at each hill he made the drunken occupants get off and push. As many of them had difficulty standing up one can understand the late arrival. The horses and brake belonged to a local coal merchant and the owner once told Fred that his horses hauled coal from Cannock Chase Collieries six days a week and were sent on the brake trips on Sundays for a rest.

There was an argument one day in the Railway Inn about the quickest way of going to Walsall and back to procure brown sugar for mixing with various drinks. Two modes of transport were available: the tramcar at half-hour intervals and the train from Birchills London and North Western Railway (LNWR) railway station situated near the Birchills tram depot. It was found out that if one caught a certain up train arriving from Rugeley for Birmingham which took five minutes to Walsall station, this left ten minutes to go to a grocer's shop specialising in brown sugar and return to board a down Birmingham to Rugeley train which took five minutes back to Birchills station. Including the short walk to and from the Railway Inn, this trip could be done in about twenty-five minutes. Going by tram to Walsall took approximately ten minutes or more each way, with a ten minute wait on The Bridge terminus. This trip therefore took thirty minutes.

As a lad playing in the vicinity of Leamore and Bloxwich Road, Fred remembers visiting a small gin pit at work. This was situated near the site of the Forest Comprehensive School and Hawley's tent works. Fred used to watch the horse walking in circles to lower men and coal up and down the mine shaft. A small tramway took the coal down to the boats at the nearby canal.

As a lad Fred Parker also used to visit the family timber yard in Green Lane via the pathway leading past the side of the tram sheds to a large house that was once part of Birchills Hall. It is believed that it was once the servant's quarters which were occupied by a relation of the Parker family, Mr Runham. The pathway ended in Green Lane opposite the Walsall Glue Works. Next to the glue works was the timber yard which was burned out in 1905. A railway siding that ran to the Birchills Hall Ironworks and the Walsall Furnaces ran across this pathway from the main Cannock line at Birchills' signal box. Fred remembers a lady being killed on the small unguarded crossing. When the new Parker timber yard was constructed after the fire, the firm acquired its own siding to accommodate large timber wagons capable of carrying a whole tree. When Fred's father decided to retire from the Railway Inn, Fred was about to leave school so he started with his two elder brothers and was to work in the timber yard until 1952. Fred recalls the constant industrial activity in Green Lane, between the canal and the railway. At night it was lit up by the eerie reflections from the glowing furnaces.

Green Lane was just a cart road and in wet weather it was almost a quagmire. Fred remembers a steam lorry overturning here. It was transporting a cargo of hams and by the time assistance arrived approximately half the hams had disappeared. Fred recalls the day the second Parker timber yard burnt down in 1905. At first Fred's two elder brothers and the workers tried to douse the fire but it was soon out of control. No telephones were available to inform the Walsall Fire Brigade, so a man set off on foot to the Bridge Street fire station. The old steam fire engine began to raise steam while the horses were fetched from Freer Street stables. They set off for the fire and arrived just in time to douse the remaining ashes of the once-busy timber yard.

Just before Fred started work, about 1907, he used to visit the Birchills Furnaces to watch the activity. The owner was a Mr Kenyon Jones and Fred was impressed by his size. He was shown over an area of Bentley Common that Jones had fenced off and then used to trap hundreds of rabbits for food for his family and workers. A railway line ran from the Birchills Furnace across the Wryley & Essington Canal to part of the common which was used for depositing large, red-hot clinkers of furnace waste. One day Fred was horrified to see a large clinker fall off a horse-drawn tub only to fall against the rear legs of the horse. The poor horse was taken back to his stable and the vet tried to save him. Fred was with the horse until he died.

In 1911 Fred and his brothers had the pleasure of a once-in-a-lifetime trip to visit the Spithead Review off the Isle of Wight, when King George V inspected the Royal Navy's fleet along with the navies of the world. They booked on a special excursion train from Walsall station to Southampton, and joined a special steamer to sail between approximately twenty miles of battleships, cruisers, destroyers and other small but important ships, so essential to the maintenance of the larger fighting ships. They finished at Portsmouth, where the train had arrived from Southampton to return them to Walsall. The railway excursion cost five shillings, with one shilling for the steamer trip. Fred had the honour of seeing the king at a distance on the bridge of the royal yacht. He recalls also the sight of the mighty German battleship *Von-Der-Tann* with all its ship's complement of officers and ratings lining the whole length of the battleship dressed in immaculate white uniforms. This trip started from Walsall late on a Friday night and arrived back at Sunday dinnertime. On the return journey in the early hours the train stopped at a small wayside station near Andover to fill its tank with water. It was a hot night and Fred put his head out of the window to sample the night air. He was rewarded by the sound of nightingales singing which, when Fred relates this trip, he says was the best five bob's worth he ever had in his life.

Fred also remembers an occasion just prior to the First World War when he was told of the arrival of a nightingale in the Bluebell Woods near the Three Crowns Hill on the way to Barr Beacon. Fred and his girlfriend, later to be his wife, had permission to stay out late one night and set off for the Three Crowns, walking from Leamore, and were rewarded by the sound of the bird. Word soon got around about this rare event and the following night many hundreds of people made the trek from the town. It was after the public houses turned out that they made their way to the Three Crowns and most of them took liquid refreshment in stone, one-gallon jars. Fred joined the crowd a few nights later but the mob must have scared the bird away with their noise. Evidently the nightingale did not choose to render his melodic evening song to a pack of beer-sodden idiots and decided to move on to a more refined audience.

An interesting part of Fred's early life was helping his Uncle Sam. Sam was a specialist breeder of Majorca fowl, which he kept on some allotments on the site of the present-day

Beeches Road and Forest Comprehensive School. Fred spent hours feeding and looking after these fowl, some 500 or more. They won prizes at shows all over England. An annual event for Fred was to exhibit some fowl at the Wolverhampton Flower Show. He carried baskets to North Walsall Midland Railway station for a train to Wolverhampton and usually returned with a prize. The flower show was always attended by large crowds and it was a pleasure to visit Wolverhampton, to mix with a fine, well-behaved class of citizen which consisted mainly of poor, working-class people.

Fred gradually began to learn the craft of woodwork at Parker's timber yard that had, by the 1920s, gained a high reputation for first class wood products. Many South Wales collieries bought regular consignments of miners' pick axe helms, whilst many famous furniture manufacturers required specially designed furniture legs. For the price of between £20-30 they could turn out four- or two-wheel carts which would be built in about ten days. The wheels were built completely by hand, for the firm had the services of a first class wheelwright who was paid the princely sum of up to £2 a week. One of the timber yard's best-selling products was the ordinary wooden wheelbarrow that sold for just five shillings. I know of one in use to this day (1982), although it had a new bottom fitted in 1950, before the timber yard closed down. Wooden supports for use in coal mines were another regular order.

It was in 1913 that Fred had an experience that was taken for granted many years ago. It was a pleasure then but today very few people would understand why. One Friday night Fred was called into the office by his elder brother and was asked if he would like a trip to Glascote Colliery near Tamworth. The purpose was to deliver wooden supports to take the place of a consignment lost on the Midland Railway. The timber yard possessed a pony and trap that was used by the brothers to visit various prospective customers around the Midlands. At 6.00 a.m. Fred loaded the pit supports onto his trap. The Parker family were proud owners of a roan mare, which was to take Fred to Tamworth. She trotted all the way at a gentle pace via Aldridge, Little Aston and Canwell. Fred recalls the tranquillity of riding along the lanes with the fresh smell of the countryside and sights of wildlife. No form of motor transport was in evidence and the trip to Tamworth was achieved by just after 10.00 a.m. It so happened that the missing railway wagon had been found and delivered one hour before Fred's arrival. The mare was fed, watered and rested as Fred had a cup of tea and a sandwich in the pit office (canteens in pits and factories were unknown in those days), and so it was a gentle trot back to Walsall arriving at 2.30 p.m.

The timber yard specialised in planks for the seventy-foot canal boats which supplied boat docks locally. Once Fred had to deliver a load of these planks to Snape's Boat Dock at Pelsall. Fred set off with a timber wagon and a pair of shire horses borrowed from a local farmer at Coal Pool. He decided to take a shortcut along Field Road to Lichfield Road. Trouble occurred at the junction, for both roads were very narrow with high hedges on either side. Whilst turning, the timber wagon got stuck fast in the banking. The only way out was to manhandle the load backwards into a suitable space to turn then go via Bloxwich.

Fred was very friendly with the Bloxwich police and often accompanied them on night patrols. One easy duty was to police from Bloxwich to the Newtown boundary in the hours of darkness as not a soul was to be seen. The policeman he remembers best was Sergeant Willets, who was very bad on his feet and was duck-footed. With his feet spread outwards, he acquired the nickname 'ten to two' after the hands of a clock. PC Yardley was a close friend of Fred and was responsible for policing Blakenall village and local farms. He was resident in the village. PCs McDonald, Cattermole and Hunt made up the rest of the force. One story concerning PC Hunt is of when a bomb fell near to the cenotaph in Walsall in 1916. He saw a tramcar arriving in Bloxwich with no lights on and a red handkerchief around the front headlight. PC Hunt stopped the driver and asked, 'Is there a fog on in Walsall?' 'No,' replied the tram driver, 'half of Walsall has been blown to bits by a German Zeppelin.' Fred Parker walked to Walsall to see the damage and remembers treading through broken glass from shattered windows in Bradford Street.

Fred used to visit a local Blakenall character named Cock Upton who ran a business from a small isolated cottage on the site of the present-day junction of Broadstone Avenue and Well Lane. This place was known as the Pop Gardens. There one could buy such beverages as nettle pop and other non-alcoholic drinks. On a warm summer's day it was well patronised by folk from Pelsall, Blakenall and Coal Pool villages, who walked along pathways over the many acres of grassland between these villages.

Into the 1920s the timber yard prospered despite the uncertain economic climate. It was on account of its efficiency and reliability that it survived. On 27 July 1927 Fred was at work amidst the circular saws and spinning shafts as the sky grew gradually dark until it was almost like night. A storm was about to burst. It was mid-afternoon and the thunder and lightning was accompanied by semi-tropical rain and hail. Inside the sawmill Fred was frightened by the vivid lightning that reflected eerily on the fast-spinning circular saw. The noise of constant thunder and the large hailstones hitting the roof made Fred think he was in Dante's Inferno. The storm raged from about 4.00 p.m. until 6.00 p.m. and as Fred returned home to his new house in Broadstone Lane he had great difficulty in walking on the hailstones, some almost one inch in circumference. Upon reaching Bloxwich Road, near Beatrice Street, the road was flooded. Several trams were stranded with no power and their wheels inches deep in hailstones. Fred went to view his Uncle Sam's fowl pens, where Beeches Road now stands. To his dismay most of the stock of prize Majorca fowl had perished in floodwater that had run down the hill to Bloxwich Road, washing away the fowl pens. It was the worst storm in Leamore in living memory, but a strange thing was that a friend of Fred's was on the canal bridge at Longwood Lane just two miles away and no rain fell, but looking towards Walsall the blackness and lightning was a most frightening sight.

During the 1930s Fred and his elder brother visited the new aerodrome between Walsall and Aldridge and once went on a sightseeing flight over Walsall to view the timber yard. There was a canal basin near the yard and the Parker brothers were in a good situation for supplying local boat builders with long planks of elm. With the railway delivering whole trees it was easy to cut them up to be loaded into canal boats. With work like this the firm managed to survive the economic depression of the 1930s. With the advent of the Second World War the Parker timber yard worked at full capacity. The government orders for office requirements – chairs, desks and tables for army, navy and air force billets – kept the firm viable. Fred Parker's two elder brothers were near retiring age but Fred was still young enough to join the police special constabulary. He served during the war years but nothing exciting happened to him. In 1946 the firm of Talbot Stead, later Tube Investments, was expanding and the land belonging to the timber yard was required for development. In 1952 the timber yard was closed down and demolished and shortly afterwards Fred's brothers passed away. For many years after, Fred could be seen walking his dog around all those parts of Leamore which have remained firm in his memory. With all the changes of modern times he was always of the opinion that it was a better life in the pre-Second World War days. Fred Parker passed away in November 1983 aged ninety-five.

Dudley Edwards, Walsall's most famous policeman

When talking to senior citizens of Walsall on the subject of the past it is surprising how many of them remember PC Dudley Edwards. Dudley Edwards was indeed a character and also a man of considerable bulk. He was over six feet tall and weighed about twenty stone. His feet and hands were almost twice the size of those of a normal man. Consequently he acquired several nicknames and was often referred to as 'Hands, feet and maulers', 'Daddy Maulers' and 'Hands across the sea'. Despite his grotesque appearance and ugly features, he was by disposition a very caring and friendly person. However, if provoked in the course of duty he was indeed a force to be reckoned with, as certain local wide boys, thieves and con men found out to their discomfort. A favourite method of Dudley's for dealing with two men for fighting was to literally grab both offenders by the scruff of the neck and bang their heads together. This procedure was always successful and quietened the dazed culprits who usually staggered off home with thick heads. This method of punishment saved Dudley from much paperwork and a court appearance (which, I am told, he would go to extreme lengths to avoid). In any case a headache was much preferred by offenders to a fine or a few days in the Goodall Street cells.

Many citizens of Walsall remember stories about Dudley Edwards. The first was related by the late Walter Holdcroft of Essex Street who, during the 1920s, acquired a job as a nightwatchman at Highgate Brewery in Sandymount Road. The first week he was on night duty, Walter made himself familiar with the premises and after the last workmen left work in the evening, he locked and secured all doors and gateways. He spent the night in a small room with a fire. The management allowed him a certain amount of beer whilst on duty, but insisted that at regular intervals he patrolled the premises. One morning about 3.00 a.m. Walter was having cheese sandwiches, along with a jar of Highgate old ale, when he heard footsteps outside. Seconds later the door crashed open and Walter was confronted by the huge frame of PC Dudley Edwards. 'How the bloody hell did you get in?' shouted Walter. 'I happen to have instructions to keep an eye on the brewery when on this beat,' said Dudley. 'You must be the new nightwatchman. As I am only on this beat every so often I did not know your predecessor had left. My presence here is not only to help security, but to have a pint of old ale and a game of cards to pass the time away.' Walter informed Dudley that he had no playing cards but had thought of buying some to play patience or solo to help break the monotony. Dudley replied, 'I will be back tomorrow night with some, so be prepared for a game,' then walked out of the room as swiftly as he came in. A few moments later Walter decided to check the security only to find every means of exit secure with no sign of any way anyone could enter or depart the Highgate Brewery. The following night Walter was dozing in a chair when Dudley Edwards crashed through the door and slung a large paper bag on his lap. Opening the bag, Walter was surprised to find the contents were about fifty packs of playing cards. 'These will last you for a time – now let's get down to a game and a pint,' said Dudley. Before he left to resume his beat Walter asked, 'How come you acquire so many packs of playing cards?' Dudley explained that on his regular patrols of back street alleyways and wasteland, almost daily he caught unemployed men passing the time away gambling for small amounts of cash. The practice was illegal but, instead of arresting these down and outs, Dudley decided the best way of dealing with them was to give them a clip round the ears and confiscate their playing cards, thus saving them a court appearance and a few days in the cells. Hence Dudley's stock of playing cards.

When on patrol in the Birchills district, Dudley Edwards often made contact with the poor working-class men who, during the Depression between the wars, found solace by sitting in groups on the grass, preferably in a hollow so as to remain unobserved. Hours were spent with playing cards, dominoes, dice and pitch and toss. Invariably gambling took place to help make the game more exciting. The stakes were a few shillings, although even these were hard to come by. One day Bill James was watching one such game beside the canal locks near Rupert Street. A group was playing pitch and toss and was oblivious to anyone who might be watching. When the concentration was at fever pitch they became aware of a shadow cast across their illegal activity. It was not the sun behind a cloud. As eyes turned upwards they saw the large portly body of Dudley Edwards. Silence prevailed for a few seconds as the gamblers began to think about their fate. Dudley slowly lowered his huge frame down to join the circle on hands and knees. Picking up the dice he said, 'Ok then blokes let's have a tuddy in'. This meant throwing the dice. After a few games Dudley was slightly in pocket so he decided to retire back to his beat leaving the lads to their illegal entertainment.

Dudley Edwards at times took his turn as duty traffic policeman on Walsall Bridge; he stood adjacent to The Bridge clock. His popularity was immense. He always had a joke for passing car drivers, tram drivers and conductors, not to mention the children as they accompanied their mothers on shopping expeditions. Fred Haywood was standing by Dunn's Tailors one day when one of the corporation steamrollers approached from Bradford Street. The steamroller driver gradually crept closer to Dudley's person. As the steaming monster was almost touching Dudley he placed his large hands against the steamroller's front wheel and bellowed to the driver, 'I'll tear you and your bloody steam roller to bits with these hands if you come another inch nearer'.

Dudley Edwards, when on night patrol in the Pleck district, was well known to the railwaymen at the New Mills Midland Railway engine shed. On the Pleck beat the routine was for the police constable to liaise with the town night patrol sergeant on the Corporation Street crossroad. The rendezvous with the sergeant, during the 10.00 p.m. till 6.00 a.m. duty, was every two hours. Dudley's favourite hour on patrol was immediately after the 2.00 a.m. meeting with the duty sergeant. After meeting the sergeant Dudley should have walked down Wednesbury Road into the Pleck and patrolled each street until the 4.00 a.m. liaison, but he had a crafty little number on this shift. He immediately set off down Wednesbury Road to visit the engine shed, situated opposite Bescot Crescent, that has long since disappeared. Sometime during the night the railwaymen had a short break whilst preparing engines for the morning passenger services. Their liquid refreshment was always a large jug of cocoa. Each night a pint can of cocoa was reserved for Dudley. His first action was on his can of cocoa, which could be boiling hot or stone cold according to the cleaning lads' availability. Hot or cold, Dudley would down the contents and proceed to lay himself horizontal on a wooden bench, giving the shed staff instructions to wake him up in time to liaise with his sergeant at Corporation Street. This memory of Dudley Edwards is from Gerald Rigby, the only survivor of Walsall's Midland Railway shed.

A story about Dudley Edwards that was told to Norris Poxon many years ago relates to an accident that was supposed to have taken place on the Chuckery beat. While Dudley was on patrol a group of excited children informed him that a horse had collapsed in Tantarra Street. When Dudley arrived on the scene he found the horse was dead. The owner had unstrapped the harness and had gone to make arrangements to move the carcass. Dudley fetched out his notebook and pencil to write out a report. After a few moments a puzzled expression appeared on his face. The notebook and pencil was returned to his pocket. Then to the amazement of a crowd of onlookers which had gathered, Dudley got hold of the horse's mane and with his immense strength proceeded to drag this unfortunate animal down Tantarra Street into Bott Lane. There he stood over the dead horse to make notes. The story goes that the reason for this behaviour was that Dudley could not spell Tantarra Street and decided to move the creature into Bott Lane as it was more easy to spell that street name. The stupidity of this story is that obviously the name of the street was engraved in large letters on each street corner and in any case policemen were not that illiterate or uneducated. This story would have been manufactured probably in one of the Chuckery public houses whilst the perpetrators of this yarn were under the influence of strong ale. Perhaps it was through a person or persons that in the past had received one of Dudley's special clouts about the cranium for some minor misdemeanour.

Mrs Ball remembers one occasion when a young courting couple were crossing a canal lock gate near her home in Canal Street to the rear of the Wolverhampton Street flour mill. The girl slipped on the damp wood of the lock gate and fell in the canal. Her boyfriend, trying to pull her out, also lost his balance and joined her in the water. The canals in those days were deep to allow constant movement of loaded coal boats. All the couple could do was to hold on to the bank and shout for someone to give them a lift up on to the towpath. As luck would have it, Dudley Edwards was passing over Wolverhampton Street canal bridge and heard cries for help. Mrs Ball and neighbours in Canal Street also heard the cries for help and reached the couple about the same time as Dudley. Mrs Ball never forgot the sight of Dudley Edwards kneeling above the unfortunate couple to grab the pair of them with his massive hands and then lift them together out of the murky canal water. Dripping wet, they thanked Dudley, who just made sure they were alright then walked them home, leaving them with a smile and telling them not to do it again and go courting in safer places.

During Dudley Edwards' time in the force there was not much vandalism, but the occasional offence did take place. One episode took place on the Caldmore beat. In most of Caldmore's back streets one could find small factories. Most of them were part of the Walsall leather industry. Fred Parker was visiting some friends one day and a solitary young lad, about twelve years old, was walking in front of him. The lad spotted a stone in the gutter and not thinking he was being observed took a shy at a leather factory's block of windows. The stone found a target and glass was shattered over the footpath. At that precise moment Fred Parker noticed a familiar figure standing motionless in an entry nearby. Yes it was the portly figure of PC Dudley Edwards. One booming shout from Dudley stopped this lad dead in his tracks and the sight of the large police uniform made him wonder what his fate would be. At the same time who should be walking along the street but the lad's mother. She watched in amazement as Dudley grabbed her son with one large hand and with the other gave the lad a hefty flick across his neck. Dudley restrained from giving the lad a good hard blow that was termed in those days 'a cogwinder', knowing full well that with his strength the lad's neck could have been broken. However, the flick was sufficient to bring tears to the lad's eyes. His mother was incensed at this treatment to her beloved offspring and proceeded to use her tongue to Dudley Edwards. After a few minutes of verbal abuse Dudley raised his voice and bellowed: 'Missus – go to bloody hell,' then walked away on his beat leaving the mother consoling her sobbing son. Some days later one of the Goodall Street sergeants told Dudley to report to Chief Inspector Ballance as soon as possible. He obliged. The police chief said, 'Edwards, I have a complaint from a lady member of the public that you hit her son and used abusive language to her person.' Dudley then explained what had happened. Mr Ballance listened intently and agreed that Dudley had done his duty as regards punishing the lad, but had left himself open to a possible court action if the said lady decided to press the matter any further. The best means of settling the problem in the Chief Inspector's view was to instruct Dudley to report to the lady in person and apologise for swearing. Fred Parker, who was a friend of Dudley Edwards and had witnessed the confrontation between Dudley and the lady, was in the know about the forthcoming visit by Dudley and decided to be on the spot to observe Dudley's method of apologising. Dudley duly arrived at the lady's house and knocked on the front door. The lady appeared at the door and for a time silence prevailed as they stood glaring at one another. Dudley suddenly said, 'Missus, do you remember what I told you to do the other day after cuffing your lad?' 'I most certainly do,' the lady replied. 'You told me to go to bloody hell.' Another silence prevailed. Then Dudley replied, 'Well you need not go there then,' and with a touch of his helmet he turned and walked away. Evidently this most unusual means of apology must have satisfied the lady as no more was heard of the situation.

After many years' loyal service, the time came for Dudley Edwards to retire. His colleagues decided to have the usual customary collection for a departing officer, but were in a quandary as to what to buy as an appropriate gift for Dudley. It was decided that Mr Ballance, the Chief Inspector, should make the decision. This he did by asking Dudley what he wanted. Mr Ballance was quite surprised at Dudley's answer. 'I want a double-barrel shotgun sir.' Mr Ballance replied, 'Your request will be granted, Edwards'. Dudley Edwards' retirement day arrived and Mr Ballance presented Dudley with a real craftsman-made double-barrel shotgun that had been purchased from a well-known sports shop which traded opposite Goodall Street police station. For some weeks after his retirement nothing was seen of Dudley Edwards. He was missed by his fellow police officers and civilians about town. Suddenly one day a knock came at the door of Mr Ballance's private residence. His wife answered the door to be confronted by Dudley Edwards who looked somewhat out of place in civilian clothes. 'Good morning madam,' said Dudley, raising his hat. 'Is the guvnor in?' 'No,' she replied, 'he is away on duty'. At that point Dudley thrust two large pheasants into her hands and said, 'Tell the guvnor to have these birds with my compliments and also tell him the shotgun is working perfect. Good day to you ma'am'.

All these tales of Dudley Edwards, probably Walsall's best-known police constable, are from local senior citizens who, when talking about the subject of Walsall's past, in all cases agreed that Dudley Edwards was always a very fair, well-liked copper. Despite his enormous size and grotesque appearance, the small children of the town almost worshipped him. Often he would hold two youngsters at shoulder height on the palms of his hand, much to the delight of their mothers. On Saturday nights after turning out time, the police had to patrol in pairs in the Green Lane and Ryecroft districts to deal with drunks who would set about a copper whilst under the influence. Dudley Edwards was often seen patrolling on his own in these areas. The thought of a swipe from those giant hands was itself a deterrent. On occasions in these districts Dudley was subject to a certain amount of cheek from older children and youths who saw fit to be amused by his grotesque features. His method of dealing with these young idiots was to remove his cape from his shoulders, spin his large frame like a shot put competitor and wade into the ruffians, scattering them like ninepins. Many senior citizens still laugh today at the memory of this human whirlwind attacking louts in this manner. It had its effect and most of these fools were loath to be on the receiving end of the swirling cape. In any case it saved Dudley arresting them and being involved in a subsequent court case. Above all, Dudley thus avoided the procedure he thoroughly detested – paperwork.

Just prior to the Second World War, various preparations took place around Walsall to cope with the emergencies that might occur in wartime. By 1938 almost every citizen was in no doubt that war with Germany was imminent. One of my first recollections was of a large army exercise that took place on what was then known as 'The Forest'. This was wasteland on the northern side of the Wyrley & Essington Canal from the old iron footbridge and Forest Brickworks over to Chestnut Road. A varied display of army Bren gun carriers, lorries, searchlights and aircraft listening devices were located in the present day (1980) Archer Road. This was not an isolated display for there were other military units within the industrial Black Country area. At night, for some weeks, aircraft flew over the Midlands. Scores of searchlights, including the Forest unit, probed the night sky to pick out the various aircraft. This attracted a vast crowd of civilian onlookers. The exercise was also a means of recruiting men for the army. Many local men enlisted in the Territorial Army and eventually gave service to their country during the following war – some with their lives.

These events passed by and during the summer of 1939 a new sight began to appear in the sky in the direction of Birmingham. The barrage balloons would be seen rising and descending at regular intervals during most days. No balloons were stationed within the Walsall boundaries. Also during the summer a lot of air force flying exercises took place. Low-flying planes, some hundreds of feet above houses, were seen frequently. I remember squadrons of Avro Ansons, Airspeed Oxfords, Bristol Blenheims, Vickers Wellingtons and also some veteran Gloster Gladiators. I do not recollect seeing any squadrons of Spitfires or Hurricanes flying at this time but did see single ones, probably on test flights. It so happened that, only a few months before war was declared, the railway took delivery of a batch of new Scammell mechanical horses. These were three-wheel articulated trucks with a payload of approximately five tons. They immediately replaced a number of the familiar horses and drays that were a feature of Walsall's railway scene.

The army made a camp at the top of Mellish Road on land to the left side of the descent down to the Dilke Arms public house. War broke out on 3 September 1939 and a few days later we cycled to Essington to see a temporary army camp complete with field kitchens and army-type bell tents in a field off Hobnock Road, just opposite the brickworks. At this time the area which is now North Walsall public works depot, off Stafford Road, was developed into a large rescue unit. Many hastily convened ambulances and rescue vans began to appear. All these vehicles were a high-class make and powerful. Many Daimlers and Lanchesters made up the fleet. Daily, these ambulances and rescue vans could be seen on training duties throughout the Walsall district. An air-raid warden's post was established in a workshop situated in the grounds of 96 Bloxwich Road. Its resident was previously Alderman McShane, JP. All local air-raid wardens for North Walsall and Ryecroft districts were trained in fire drill, first aid and civil defence routine here. Most streets had a resident warden who was identified by a sign on his particular residence. This post was manned twenty-four hours a day. Firewatchers were also on continual alert.

With the war now on, all we children were to report back to North Walsall School about the second week in September. On the appointed day we assembled in our new classes to be greeted by our headmaster, Mr Ash of the senior school, to be told to go home until further notice. The government had passed a resolution that no child must go to school until all air-raid shelters had been constructed for the safety of all staff and pupils. This procedure applied to all Walsall schools. The extra holiday was very much appreciated but owing to the fear of air raids and the method of war – then an unknown quantity – all children had to play close to their own homes.

In the event, going back to school took place in about February or March 1940. Christmas had arrived by the time air-raid shelters were constructed. Then the schools of Walsall became victims of one of the worst winters within living memory. Deep snow and temperatures well below zero prevailed for most of January and February. A grave coke and fuel shortage, along with burst pipes, rendered classrooms uninhabitable until heat was restored.

A few days before the Second World War broke out, a familiar sight occurred in Walsall's residential streets. This was the sight of LMS railway lorries delivering Anderson air-raid shelters to every household. At Long Street goods depot trains arrived at regular intervals with the familiar corrugated, galvanised steel shelters. One must give credit to the government of the day for their swift distribution of the Anderson shelters. If you visited any household back garden when the shelters arrived, one could, after working hours, find men digging holes and erecting shelters.

There was no complacency in those days, as most citizens had seen cinema newsreels a few years previously of the new style of aerial warfare during the Spanish Civil War. Many male householders who were rearing families had served in the First World War so they were under no illusions as to what the future could hold. Despite this it was surprising how citizens made the spartan accommodation of these Andersen shelters into a place to live in. In any case, after many houses had been blitzed, they were to be home for a considerable time. During the long winter nights of 1940 and 1941 most Webster Road citizens slept all night in these Anderson shelters as there were air-raid warnings most nights. They were reasonably comfortable mainly thanks to the housewives who somehow managed to drape curtains and cloths around the bunk beds. Some citizens laid an electric cable from the house while others made do with candles and torches. Condensation was a problem when sleeping there all night. I well remember waking in the morning to look up and see drops of water from the galvanised sheets falling on the beds. Most shelters were heated by Valor paraffin stoves. Fortunately there were ample supplies of paraffin available in the many local shops. It was with a certain amount of

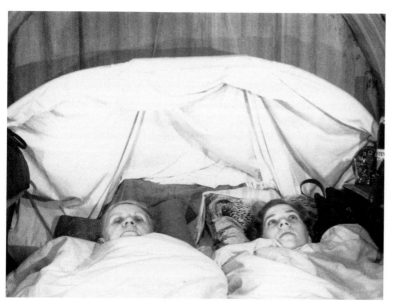

Anderson air-raid shelter, c. 1940-1941. These corrugated, galvanized steel shelters were delivered to every household just before the Second World War broke out. The household was responsible for erecting them. During 1940 and 1941 people slept in the shelters most nights because of air-raid warnings. As shown here, most people tried to make the shelters as comfortable as possible.

pride that many people grew flowers on top of the shelters whilst the rest of our gardens were filled with vegetables.

In 1940, just before the Germans invaded the Low Countries and France, a regular flow of special troop trains were seen by many schoolchildren and the few adults who were about. By this time all men who had not been called up for military service were working very long hours. Many troopships were arriving at Liverpool with soldiers from Great Britain's dominions. It was customary for engines to be changed in Walsall station after running from Liverpool. Engines from the Midland Division transported troops to hastily erected camps in the eastern and southern parts of England. Tea was provided on Walsall station by local soldiers from the South Staffordshire Regiment, based in Whittimere Street drill hall, as the engines were changed and carriage roof tanks filled with water. Our viewpoint for these troop specials was the Mill Lane bridges at Ryecroft. As the locomotives toiled up to Lichfield Road Junction, Anzacs complete with bush hats waved to us children and threw coins to us. South Africans and Rhodesians, along with Canadians, did the same, much to the delight of the local children. Some of these specials detrained at Sutton Park station and, for a time, some thousands of troops were camped in the park. On the climb from Ryecroft Junction to Lichfield Road Junction I well remember two trains which consisted of vintage LNWR stock, including many twelve-wheel carriages, such was the demand for rolling stock. The two locomotives hauling these trains were No. 6134 *The Cheshire Regiment* and No. 5675 *Hardy*. Walsall's railway system was just about running to capacity during those dark days of 1940 and 1941.

There was constant activity at the Walsall Civil Defence Headquarters in North Walsall, which was based off the Stafford Road where the public works depot is now. All the rescue vans and ambulances were running around Walsall on training exercises. Houses that were condemned would be used for this training and field kitchens erected, in preparation for the real thing. With the advent of Dunkirk the war became more real to Walsall citizens, after the period known as the phoney war. Walsall experienced little enemy action compared with other English towns. However, certain small events did occur. Us lads from North Walsall School who could boast the possession of a cycle began to visit these. At the time our parents gave us latitude and the freedom to travel. My father's main advice during 1940 and 1941 was to return home immediately upon hearing church bells ringing. All church bells during the Second World War adhered to government instructions to remain silent, only to be rung if an invasion of England took place.

I cannot remember the exact dates of the first few bombs to drop on the Walsall area. The first I remember affected the Walsall Golf Club and the Broadway ring road when bombs straddled the road blowing a number of roofs off. Bomb craters were made in ploughed fields which are now the site of the West Midland College. From this event we procured our first war souvenirs, which were shrapnel from the burst bombs.

About this time, when the air raids began to concentrate on Birmingham and Coventry, our family became firm friends with the Cooper family who lived at 84 Webster Road. Mr and Mrs Cooper had two sons, Carl and George, and a daughter, Madge. We decided to lift the gloom of shelter life by installing a telephone between our respective air-raid shelters. It transpired that a junk shop in George Street had quantities of redundant phones, earphones and crystal radio sets. For about two shillings and sixpence we acquired a job lot of this equipment including many yards of wiring. Soon we had a line established between our air-raid shelters and also between George Cooper's bedroom and my bedroom with the lines tied along the house spouting. Our family had an old-fashioned wind-up gramophone. When we tied the speaker to the gramophone earpiece with string (this was before the age of Sellotape), we could broadcast to No. 84's shelter. All this was very crude. Records were purchased from various junk shops and market stalls. They were of 1920s vintage and today would be collectors' items but were sold to us for the princely sum of one penny each. Our favourites for some unknown reason were the Scots Guards playing *Sons of the Brave* and *Colonel Bogey*. There was also a record of two waltzes, *Estudantina* and *Espana*, and one that was popular with our mothers which contained *In a Monastery Garden* and *In a Persian Market*. Often during an air raid we would be listening to the quiet birdsong from *In a Monastery Garden* at the same time as we heard the thud of anti-aircraft shells exploding over Birmingham.

Our family and the Cooper family, like most of Webster Road's residents, began to organise visits to each other's homes and shelters. About this time Marks and Spencer's store in Walsall sold dartboards for two shillings and sixpence and regular dart matches took place. Sometimes, although an air-raid warning had sounded, we would play in the houses until almost daybreak, whilst our fathers, the breadwinners, slept in the shelter to gain strength for a ten- or twelve-hour shift. While we played our darts, there was always the drone of German aircraft above us with the familiar sound of their de-synchronized engines which identified them from our own aircraft. We learned many years later that this practice was used to put fear into the civilian population and I can well remember several local ladies being most apprehensive during air raids.

Each time Birmingham suffered an air raid most of us children retired to the sand hole situated at the top of Webster Road and Essex Street. From this point we had a grandstand view over Birmingham. If there was a full moon we could see German bombers crossing the moon face. I now know, after reading the book *Most Secret War* by Professor R.V. Jones, that the wireless knickbeams beamed from the Continent to Birmingham terminated over Walsall from the direction of Perry Barr. After the bombers had unloaded their deadly cargo on Birmingham, the planes then circled over Walsall to return to their bases in France. Looking back, with hindsight we were acting in sheer stupidity, watching Birmingham being bombed, for in the sky were the twinkling flashes of hundreds of anti-aircraft shells exploding. Grown ups, as well as children, took part in this folly and no one possessed a steel hat. The following morning the streets were, in places, lined with shrapnel. My father, who spent four years in France with the Royal Garrison Artillery, did point out to me and the Cooper family that some of the anti-aircraft shells were fired from the south of Birmingham, reaching a height of some 10,000 feet before exploding. He stressed to us the fact that if one of them failed to explode it would land in the vicinity of Walsall. A few nights afterwards, his warning was brought home to us. We were walking up the Cooper's garden path on the way to the shelter as the barrage had become so intense that we had curtailed our darts match. There was a sudden and terrifying shriek that nearly deafened us and, with an instant reaction, made us all dive face down into the garden's potato plot. We all expected a mighty explosion but to sustained relief one did not come. It transpired that an anti-aircraft shell had landed in the next street, Beddows Road, and had failed to explode. All I remember was a hole near the gate of No. 22 Beddows Road with flagstones scattered in all directions. A man had been standing by this gate and had unfortunately been killed by the shell. The ARP rescue van with a policeman arrived sometime after the event and in no time dispersed all onlookers and instructed all people in the nearby streets to remain in their shelters. The reason the emergency services did not arrive on the scene at once was that no householders during the 1940s were affluent enough to have a phone installed.

Presentation of ARP van by Walsall Co-op Society. By May 1938 Walsall had recruited 250 air-raid precautions wardens. There was supposed to be one warden per street and a name plate was fixed to his house. One of the many duties of the wardens was to maintain the blackout regulations.

The nearest phone boxes were on Bloxwich Road and at Coal Pool. If, in an emergency, one had to use these public phones they were always in working order. No children or youths were involved in vandalism in those days.

During 1940 and 1941 I assisted Mrs Cooper's mother and father, who were then past retiring age, and who held the post of steward and stewardess of the social club for the large Walsall leather firm of Handford Greatrex Ltd. Mr Tom Bathurst was a retired, self-employed leather worker who specialised in harnesses for the horse trade. His wife was a typical Victorian lady who, with her husband, lived a life of true principles, dedication and honesty with faith in religion. The club was situated on the fourth floor of No. 19 Bridge Street, Walsall. The clubroom was about 100 feet long with three snooker tables and one bagatelle table. Owing to wartime conditions the club was only open on Friday evenings and Saturday and Sunday lunchtime and evening. Looking back, this club was situated in a most ridiculous place, for any visitor had to climb four sets of stone stairs and anyone who was drunk late at night would have had difficulty getting down. All supplies of barrelled or bottled beer and pop had to be manhandled up these stairs. The delivery draymen were responsible for the beer barrels, but the crates of bottled pop, beer and stout were left to Mr Bathurst. George and Madge Cooper and myself came in useful for our Saturday morning assistance. We were responsible for the primitive heating system for the club. It consisted of about two dozen Valor paraffin oil stoves. In a yard to the rear of the building was situated a one hundred-gallon paraffin tank adjacent to the Ford Brook before it disappeared under the bridge. We carried two stoves at a time up the four flights of stairs on this task. On Saturday nights we used to stay at the club until almost midnight then accompany Mr and Mrs Bathurst back home to their residence, No. 154 Portland Street. One Saturday night a heavy air raid was in progress with Birmingham the target. We heard shrapnel hitting the roof above and not many customers remained until closing time. It was pitch dark when we left the club, only to find an ARP warden sheltering in the doorway. He advised us not to make our way home, but we decided to take a chance. We made our way to the bus stop by Sister Dora's statue to await one of the petrol buses coming off service on the long-distance routes, as the trolleybus to

Wartime fundraising event. There was a great deal of fundraising for the war effort. Among Walsall campaigns were War Weapons Week which successfully raised money to buy a destroyer and the Wings for Victory week which provided money for Sunderland planes.

Bloxwich had departed. The empty buses returning to Birchills depot would always pick up spare passengers as far as the depot, unlike today's drivers who would not. Mr and Mrs Bathurst left the bus at the Blue Lane stop and we alighted at North Walsall. How the bus conductors managed to work in such nocturnal conditions I shall never know. The bus interior lights were shaded almost to nil visibility. The only aid was a specially designed flash lamp attached to the conductor's uniform which was just sufficient for him to see the coins and tickets.

Helping and assisting elderly people was a regular feature of life for us children during the war; our parents insisted on this. One morning after an air raid that affected Darlaston, we were asked to cycle to All Saints Road to see if some relatives of our neighbour's were alright after we had heard of bombs in the vicinity. The news reached us via factory workers coming off the night shift from the complex of factories engaged in war work along the Walsall to Darlaston Road. One must remember that in 1940-45 no working-class people possessed a telephone nor was there any local radio in those days. We cycled post-haste to All Saints Road to find our friends safe, but we witnessed the sad sight of All Saints church completely gutted and still on fire after receiving a direct hit.

During the uncertain times of 1940 and 1941 we children of North Walsall still enjoyed a certain amount of freedom. We were still allowed to cycle to Lichfield Trent Valley station for trainspotting as we had done pre-war. There were extra trains running conveying materials previously unknown to us, such as a trainload of magnetic mines on the move, from the many shadow factories that had sprung up nationwide, to British naval bases. Only a few miles along the A461 road that crossed the main line in the direction of Burton-on-Trent was situated Fradley Aerodrome. We found it a very pleasant diversion from trainspotting to cycle to the canal at Fradley and ride along the towpath which gave us a grandstand view of some very rare aircraft and their activities. Fradley was a flying training school, repair and maintenance depot. Planes were taking off and landing every few minutes. To us young lads, a sixteen-mile cycle ride to see hundreds of steam engines and the same number of aircraft was an adventure and the sort of

Captured ME 109, Walsall Arboretum, 1940. The aircraft was on display to raise money for the Walsall Spitfire Fund. The fund was one of the first to raise money for the war effort. The organizers sent £11,000 to the Minister of Aircraft Production in November 1940 for purchase of two Spitfires and gave the balance of about £650 to the Royal Air Force Benevolent Fund.

excitement denied to today's youngsters in this age of television and electronic gimmicks. Always in the direction of Fradley, one could see planes circling around like hornets above a jam pot. The most common aircraft was the Vickers Wellington.

One morning on arrival at Lichfield Trent Valley station we joined about fifty trainspotters to begin our stint of collecting train numbers, when two spotters arrived on their cycles (all spotters came by bike, many from far away, to this railway mecca). They had come from Derby and gave us the exciting news that a Wellington Bomber had landed in the canal. Soon a cavalcade of cyclists was speeding down the Burton Road then onto the canal towpath. We were not allowed to go near the aircraft, which was guarded by Air Force police, but we saw what had happened. Evidently the bomber's brakes had failed upon landing. It had overshot the runway and crashed through a hedge. Its undercarriage wheels were firmly embedded in the canal. As we left to go back to Lichfield Trent Valley station, several coal boats were forming a queue and feverish activity was taking place to haul the Wellington back on the field.

Another interesting event relating to the Fradley Wellington Bombers happened while I was watching the trains blasting their way through Lichfield Trent Valley station. It was the sight of a Wellington Bomber above us displaying a large circular de-gauzing ring that was on trial to deal with a new German invention, the magnetic mine. The joke soon went around the trainspotters that Wellington Bombers were so good they sported a halo. Another surprise took place during yet another trainspotting expedition when we heard a roar of aircraft engines different from the Wellingtons, Ansons and Tiger Moths we had become so used to. From behind the imposing structure of the Trent Valley maltings rose our first sighting of a four-engine Short Stirling Bomber. It was the first four-engine aircraft we had seen and on arrival back home and at North Walsall School no one believed us, but within a year they were a familiar sight over Walsall.

Back in Walsall, we children had to do regular errands for our parents, especially visiting shops to get extra food, as the rationing was beginning to cause mother some headaches. We used to walk to various farms in order to purchase eggs or fruit. A typical dinner for me was a cup of weak tea along with about four rounds of dry bread and one apple, sliced. Sometimes the bread would have a smear of butter or margarine.

Alternatively, jam was our standard dinner. In winter mother would manage to make soup from the remnants of the Sunday dinner or by foraging in our butcher's, which happened to be Dawsons of Stafford Street, where a few meat scraps could be purchased at an opportune moment. A most amusing sight to us children, but not to local working men, was their antics during the beer shortage. Like all commodities during the war, beer was rationed out to pubs. Publicans decided to stagger their opening hours, which resulted in the sight of as many as thirty or more men waiting outside the pub for the gaffer to open up. In the case of Stafford Street, from the start at Town End Bank to the turning off for Hospital Street there were no fewer than twelve public houses. As one pub ran out of beer and another opened its doors one could see some fifty or so men on the run, which reminded one of animals stampeding. The local breweries, at about this time, experimented with a brew that must have had a substitute for hops or was watered down somewhat. My father was of the opinion that it was made with the aid of some chemical formula. One must remember this was the time of the Battle of Britain, which resulted in labour shortages in the Kent hop fields. This substitute brew acquired the nickname of 'Smackers' among local working men.

Our fathers also had problems with cigarette supplies, which were on a sort of unofficial ration from shopkeepers, who did their best to serve their regular, pre-war customers. What affected us children was that cigarette cards ceased to be printed and this was the end of a very pleasant hobby for children collecting them. Sadly they were not revived after hostilities ceased. Most of our fathers smoked cigarettes. My father, like most of the working class, preferred the Wills Woodbines, Gold Flake, Navy Cut or Players. These brands were cheaper and suited the working man's pocket in contrast to rich upper-class smokers who could afford the brands of Kensitas (which, incidentally, gave away silk-lined pictures, in contrast to the common cigarette card), Craven A and Park Drive. Like the 'Smackers' for beer drinkers, a substitute appeared in the cigarette shops, a brand known as 'Bar 1'. Most men I knew said they tasted horrible, but to the habitual smoker they were better than none. The joke got around that these cigarettes were made from the sweepings up from the tobacco factories' floors.

One morning at North Walsall, our school studies were interrupted by the air-raid siren, otherwise known to us children as 'Moaning Minnie'. In record time the whole school was below the playgrounds. We all heard a low-flying aircraft pass above, to be followed by a thud. We found out later that two bombs had dropped on Walsall gas works, one failing to explode. Eyewitnesses aboveground clearly saw the German bomber passing above our school. Another near miss was a stick of bombs falling on the 'Swags'. This today is the sight of Walsall's public works depot and the MEB (Midlands Electricity Board) offices in Green Lane. One bomb failed to explode and, when the army bomb disposal unit arrived to explode it, the whole of North Walsall School had to retire to the shelters. At the precise time it blew up there was an accompaniment of cheers from all the pupils.

We made a few more cycle trips to visit barrage balloon sites. The one in West Bromwich Dartmouth Park was easy to view. We had our first sight of women in uniform here with almost the whole unit being manned by WAAFs. Another one was situated in a sand quarry at Queslet.

The day after the famous air raid on Coventry, I decided to cycle there to witness the damage, unknown to my parents, who thought I was trainspotting. Once past Meriden, I caught the first sight of enemy action, a small garage almost burnt out and on the road a once-proud new Leyland Tiger coach still blazing away. I reached the Coventry bypass and from this point to the city centre problems arose. Most of the highway was festooned with

Above left: *Cutting from the* Walsall Observer, *6 January 1940. Rationing was officially introduced on 8 January 1940. Meat rationing did not begin until March, but people had been warned earlier to register with a butcher. Everyone over six got one shilling and ten pence worth of meat a week and eleven pence worth for younger children. The adult meat ration varied, but as late as three weeks after VE Day, May 1945, it was still only one shilling and two pence. (Reproduced by courtesy of the* Walsall Observer.*)*

Centre: *Cutting from the* Walsall Observer, *13 January 1940. Bread was not rationed until after the war. The Walsall Co-op Society was, however, helping the war cause by not using lights or power at night. (Reproduced by courtesy of the* Walsall Observer.*)*

Above right: *Cutting from the* Walsall Observer, *20 January 1940. One of the films produced to support the government's Grow More Food campaign was shown at St Paul's Hall, Walsall. The organizers apologized for the lack of advertising because the number of posters they could use was limited. By 1942 there were 3,000 public allotments in the borough with some 550 in parks and playing fields. (Reproduced by courtesy of the* Walsall Observer.*)*

fire hoses lined up to the many factories still on fire from the previous night's holocaust. The only traffic in sight consisted of fire engines and ARP rescue vans. I got to a position where I could just see the burnt-out shell of Coventry Cathedral when a policeman enquired if I was looking for someone. When I told him I had just cycled from Walsall he immediately gave me my marching orders to return home at once, stressing the fact that the Germans could pay a daylight visit. I returned home with the smell of burning in my nostrils and a memory I shall never forget. On the way home I stopped to watch trains at Castle Bromwich. Every few minutes, trains full of war produce would be on the move in between the well-patronised passenger trains. From the nearby aerodrome came the constant roar of aero engines from a variety of aircraft, including Spitfires, Hurricanes, Defiants and Wellingtons. When I finally arrived home father enquired about my absence and did not believe me about my expedition. When he realised what I had done I received a very stern lecture and was advised to keep away from built-up cities. However we still did occasional sorties into Birmingham after air raids.

One of our pleasures during wartime was visits to Walsall's eight cinemas. To see a cinema show was quite an achievement as most cinemas were full to capacity from about 6.00 p.m. It was most amusing to see the workers disgorging from Walsall's factories between 5.00 and 6.00 p.m. Some would go direct to the cinema from work without any tea, others would go home on a grossly overloaded bus, rush into home, swallow a quick tea and go back into town to join a cinema queue and, if in luck, would manage to see the main film, starting about 8.30 p.m. In our part of Walsall I well remember the wartime factory exodus up Stafford Street. Trolleybuses and petrol buses would be seen crawling to Leamore and Bloxwich slowed down by literally thousands of pedal cyclists. Sometimes, when in a rush to get to the cinema, we would go on cycles. We simply deposited our cycles in cycle racks on a car park devoid of cars owing to part-time petrol rationing. It was a regular occurrence to be watching a film when on the screen a caption was superimposed announcing 'Air raid warning'. I do not remember anyone leaving or any kind of panic.

Wending our way by either walking, cycling or by bus on a cloudy night in total blackout conditions was an adventure in itself, but the majority of people bumping into one another would all be laughing and joking. It can be said that amongst these working-class people walking through Walsall on their way home from dances or the pictures, no muggings or vandalism took place. From a Saturday night dance young girls would go home in complete safety, intermingling with men from all three services, including many Dutch servicemen billeted near Wolverhampton. The last train from Walsall station to Rugeley was always full to capacity in the early years of the war, first with the Fleet Air Arm and later Royal Air Force men stationed at Brindley Heath, near Hednesford. The Walsall station concourse would be packed with girls seeing their servicemen off to camp. The only trouble was with those in a high state of intoxication.

The station entrance in Station Street was also busy with servicemen and ladies of easy virtue from the dark streets of Marsh Street, Lower Marsh Street and Marsh Lane. All this low life was centred in the area of the Dun Cow public house in Wolverhampton Street. About this time I remember another air raid that was close enough to make us retire to the safety of our shelters. A dull thud was heard. It transpired that it was a solitary bomb landing in soft soil adjacent to a building in Hospital Street. Unfortunately, three men on firewatching duties were killed.

I left North Walsall School at the age of fourteen in October 1941 and immediately started work at Birchills bus depot. Although I have stated that people were happy with wartime life, this was only to a certain extent. Deep down, most people, especially the older ones, were very apprehensive about the future as we experienced one setback after another. Then, on 6 December, America entered the Second World War. A tremendous relief swept through schools, factories and homes. I remember my father arriving home for tea and telling mother and myself that we would be safe in our lifetime. He told me that it was now a very remote possibility that I would hear church bells ringing whilst on my cycling trips warning of the impending German invasion.

Another interesting episode in our trainspotting activities was the regular visits to Bushbury shed, Wolverhampton. I had an uncle and auntie living in Sherbourne Road, very near the engine shed where Uncle Harry Poyner worked as a main line fireman. We lads all used to sit on a large fence overlooking the shed, which always had a cloud of smoke over it from the constant procession of engines working to full wartime capacity. The nearby sidings by the Goodyear tyre factory were filled with loads of

Second World War Home Guard members at the transport depot, North Walsall. Like all those exempt from war service because of their work or age, the depot staff had to join the Home Guard. The Walsall Home Guard exercised regularly with one unit from one area trying to infiltrate another area. They were stood down in December 1944.

essential war products, awaiting movement north or south. From up in the sky came the ceaseless drone of Tiger Moth training aircraft twisting and turning in considerable numbers. A number of Boulton and Paul Defiants could also be seen on test. We visited the Wolverhampton Aerodrome often and anyone under the age of forty-five could not imagine the activity that took place because of Wolverhampton's contribution to the war effort. Our trips to and from Bushbury were via Blackhalve Lane and Essington. That took us over three level crossings carrying the mineral lines for Holly Bank and Hilton main collieries. Judging by the number of times we were held up to let the trains pass, the local miners did their share for the war effort.

As I have said, during the autumn of 1941 I left school to commence work at Birchills bus depot. This meant less time for cycle rides but every available moment that could be spared was taken to observe the changing local situation. For one thing the Yanks were about to invade England. A few troop trains began to be seen passing Ryecroft Junction full of GIs. It was while we were waiting for one of these troop specials that we heard a new sound from the main Lichfield Road direction. We immediately pedalled to investigate and were thrilled to see our first tank, which I believe was a Valentine. It transpired that, owing to the war in the Western Desert of North Africa, the manufacture of tanks became a priority and orders for these tanks were given to the Patent Shaft Company of Wednesbury.

The reason for tanks rattling through Walsall was to test them for desert conditions. The most suitable areas for these tests were the sand pits near Shire Oak and Canwell, near Sutton. I well remember one of these monsters approaching The Bridge from Bradford Place with The Bridge traffic policeman standing well back from the spinning tracks. It clattered by Sister Dora's statue complete with its lethal gun, passing the Town Hall, where, incidentally, one of the first tanks ever made was on display in 1916 to raise money for the First World War. Another noise that became familiar to Walsall citizens from 1942 onwards was caused by the testing of North American Harvard training aircraft that had been repaired at Helliwells factory on Walsall Aerodrome. The Pratt and Whitney radial engine was probably the most noisy aircraft engine about at this time and Walsall citizens had to put up with its constant drone from the sky until well after the Second World War.

Walking through Walsall at this time it was commonplace to see a fair number of the population in uniform. On a visit to the pictures one would see factory and shop girls accompanied not only by army, navy and air force men but also Poles, Czechs and Dutch servicemen and later the town was almost overrun by Yanks. One Sunday evening, I well remember, was spent in the Empire Cinema in Freer Street, when, at about 7.00 p.m., superimposed on the screen while we were watching a film called *The Great Barrier* about the building of the Canadian Pacific Railway, was the sign 'Air raid warning'. When the film ended we came out of the dimly lit cinema vestibule to be greeted with the sound of bursting anti-aircraft shells and the usual bits of shrapnel falling. A number of RAF personnel from Hednesford gave us the encouragement to chance our luck and press on home regardless. It happened that a heavy raid on Birmingham was in progress. We crossed Albert Street footbridge, which was engulfed in smoke from a north-bound mineral train. Looking towards the Town Hall one could see the searchlights probing the night sky, intermingled with bursting shells. To our right was the well-known Walsall foundry of Goodwins, situated in the Wisemore and Duncalfe Street area. Suddenly we saw sparks flying as shrapnel ricocheted from the foundry's steel roof. We decided to run for shelter in the doorway of the foundry and for once George and Madge Cooper and myself were somewhat scared and we remained under shelter for some time before proceeding to run home as fast as possible.

One night in 1942 Walsall suffered its worst air raid. Early evening the sirens sounded and many German planes passed over, heading north. About midnight we received the all-clear siren, but decided to remain in our shelter. At about 4.00 a.m. the warning sounded again. As my father and myself had to report to work at Birchills bus depot within a few hours, we decided to get up and look outside. I remarked to my father, 'Hark at that heavy rain falling in the distance,' fully expecting to get drenched any minute. 'That's no rain,' my father replied, 'It must be incendiary bombs'. It transpired that he was right, for over a thousand incendiaries fell in the vicinity of Bloxwich Road and Birchills bus depot. After about ten minutes the sky was lit up as the incendiaries found their mark. We were informed later that the bombers we heard earlier were on their way to attack Liverpool and on the return trip some of their planes had surplus bombs still aboard and passing over Walsall saw the inviting structures of Talbot Stead's tube works and Birchills bus depot. We all decided to stay in our shelters for a time, fully expecting some high-explosive bombs to be jettisoned into the chaos caused by the fire bombs, but to our relief no more planes were heard and the Germans must have retired back to France as daylight was near.

The all-clear sounded and some of us ventured on to Rutland Street railway bridge to see Hawley's tent works ablaze. The whole of the grass railway bank near Forest Lane was burning furiously and I saw several of the railway telephone poles on fire and falling amid a shower of sparks across the main Cannock line. Returning home to have some breakfast before going to work, there was another glow in the sky that came from the Butts district. It transpired that Hawley's other firm had received a stick of incendiary bombs and was completely gutted like its parent firm in Bloxwich Road. Number two bay of Birchills depot was also ablaze and from this inferno a Home Guard man on duty, Corporal Kitson, a bus driver, drove seven flaming buses onto the apron by the nearby ticket office, but unfortunately the fire brigade and auxiliary service were too busy attending to number one bay to deal with them. In this bay were one diesel and four petrol pumps containing thousands of gallons of fuel. By a miracle a great explosion was averted, but residents of Bloxwich Road were temporarily evacuated by the police.

Hints on WAR-TIME SPENDING AND SAVING

Here are three ships

1 This one is loaded with foodstuffs and necessaries

2 This one is loaded with munitions

3 This one is loaded with unnecessary goods

By limiting your purchases of the goods contained in Ship No. 3, you leave more cargo space for the goods we need to win the war. Spend carefully then—buy what you must—but avoid spending on unnecessary things, particularly goods which come from abroad.

Result :

(1) *You increase the shipping available for essentials.*

(2) *You have more money to invest in National Savings Certificates and the New Defence Bonds.*

HOW TO LEND TO HELP WIN THE WA

1. National Savings Certificates *Free of Income Tax.* Price 15s. Value after 5 years 17s. 6d. After 10 years 20s. 6d., which equals interest at £3 3s. 5d. per cent. Maximum holding 500 Certificates including earlier issues.

2. 3% Defence Bonds £5 and multiples of £5. Income Tax NOT deducted at source. Maximum

3. Post Office Savings Bank a Trustee Savings Banks. Any sum from 1s. upwards w annual limit of £500.

★ To Employers and Employ Has a National Savings Group b formed in your office, works or sho If not, write at once to the Natio Savings Committee, London, S.W Savings Groups provide the b and easiest method of accumula

Cutting from the Walsall Observer, *20 January 1940. National savings certificates were one of many ways used to raise money for war funds. In 1943 the* Wings for Victory *week in Walsall which raised money to buy Sunderland planes used this amongst other fundraising methods. (Reproduced by courtesy of the* Walsall Observer.*)*

When I arrived for work all that was left of the seven buses, including numbers 87, 113, 179, 180, 192 and 205, were their twisted chassis. Corporal Kitson might just as well have left them in number two bay. However he did qualify for a medal for his efforts. Over the whole of the depot premises, we found hundreds of incendiary bombs that had been extinguished with sandbags plus many that had failed to explode. The local Home Guard and firewatchers probably saved the whole of Birchills bus depot from being destroyed. In spite of the destruction, approximately fifty per cent of the buses entered service that morning, but to my knowledge no one received any thanks for their efforts in preventing a serious fire or at least trying to run a bus service for the war workers. Within a few days, the deficiency in buses was made up by a loan of buses from London Transport and Manchester Corporation plus some motor coaches of the holiday trade. It certainly surprised local people to see these red-coloured Crossley buses running on all Walsall routes and particularly the London Transport AEC Regents with their open staircases.

About this time until just after D-Day in June 1944, Walsall saw a most varied and interesting display of aerial activity above the town. Most North Walsall schoolboys who were dedicated trainspotters now added to their excitement by spotting the many new types of aircraft, including the American planes that were filtering in in vast quantities with the impending invasion of the Continent. One evening after finishing work, as I made my way to Ryecroft engine shed, coming from over St Matthew's church and passing directly over the rows of smoking locomotives was a Consolidated Catalina Flying Boat that looked very much out of place in our industrial Midlands. We also saw occasional Short Sunderland Flying Boats. What their business was so far inland we never found out.

When the Yanks gradually began to set up air bases in England, we lads had a great time looking out for aircraft. Hundreds passed over Walsall each day, but the sight of Boeing B17s Flying Fortresses was something I shall never forget. It made us feel very secure and gave hope for the future. Vast numbers of Liberators and also Wellingtons, Stirlings, Halifaxes and Lancasters passed overhead. At this time England was more or less one large aerodrome. One Sunday afternoon in the late summer of 1943, my one free day from work, I decided to cycle to Castle Bromwich to see the activity at this famous aerodrome. At the same time the busy Midland Railway line was, even on Sundays, moving traffic on a scale that would shame today's normal midweek service. Looking down from the station bridge was the large factory of Fisher and Ludlow that had been turned over to the manufacture of Spitfires and Lancasters. From the direction of the aerodrome came the sounds of aircraft engines revving up and a Spitfire above going through a series of aerobatics in the hands of a test pilot. It could have been Alec Henshaw, the famous pre-war aviator who was resident chief test pilot at Castle Bromwich.

It was about teatime on this Sabbath and many people would be about to visit their respective churches, but I was suddenly reminded there was still a war on. A tractor came from the direction of the aerodrome, crossed the main road then proceeded towards the aircraft factory. The tractor driver dismounted and disappeared through a small doorway. Then the large hangar doors slowly began to open to reveal the magnificent sight of a Lancaster Bomber fresh off the assembly line with others behind almost complete. The tractor then began to tow the Lancaster across the main road. The sight of this monster crossing the Chester Road can never be forgotten. Traffic was very sparse in wartime but a few cars had to wait while this giant was slowly towed to the aerodrome. I often wonder what happened to this one particular Lancaster I saw, but this event took place several times a day. So I returned home pausing at Erdington to watch a few tramcars which, about this time, were doing great business, taking men of the three services back to their camps after thirty-six- or forty-eight-hour passes.

Sundays were the one wartime day civilians could afford some pleasure. One hot summer day with two of my neighbours, Mary Taylor and Joan Freeman, I decided to cycle to Bridgenorth. There was an abundance of cyclists on the road with the same idea. The number 17 bus service from Wolverhampton to Bridgenorth was normally a one-hour service, but Wolverhampton Corporation somehow found extra fuel to run many specials for people on war work, who had worked twelve-hour shifts for six days, to have a break. As we cycled along we heard the familiar sound of the Gardner engine COG 5 Daimler buses of Wolverhampton Corporation behind us and as they passed the passengers seemed to be happy. This resulted in exchanges of waving and shouts of 'Keep pedalling' to us. Bridgenorth was crowded with people, but very few motor cars were in evidence. Many of our forces and a few GIs, all with girlfriends, strolled around the town. The funicular railway to Hightown was working to capacity. Many shops were open for tea, pop and ice cream. This had a taste unlike pre-war, owing to wartime rationing of sugar, but still the traders did a roaring trade.

We returned home after tea and approaching Wolverhampton, near Shipley, we heard the roar of a bomber. To our surprise it was a B17 Flying Fortress, flying only a few hundred feet up at right angles to us. It had obviously just returned from some operation, for most of one side of the fuselage had been shot away and standing inside its gaping hole were two Yanks viewing our English countryside. It flew in the direction of Cosford Aerodrome, but could have been trying to land at the nearby Halfpenny Green Aerodrome that was made famous by the film *The Way to the Stars*. Thus we returned home after enjoying a pleasant afternoon and evening during wartime.

In 1943 and 1944 people began to see the light at the end of the tunnel, after the dark days of 1940, 1941 and 1942. From now on Walsall was to have an invasion of Americans that lasted up until D-Day, 6 June 1944. One day I was visiting my father at the Tramway Club in Stafford Street, then situated where the new law courts are now. The building next door was the new Catholic church hall. American Army trucks were outside delivering beds and cooking utensils and by the following day some fifty or more GIs had made it home and were there for about six months. A few weeks later the recreation field near Butts Bridge, known as Rue Meadow, that used to be owned by an ex-mayor, Peter Bull, became a camp for the American Motor Transport Company. Approximately 500 GIs were billeted in large bell tents and their presence did not go unnoticed by local females.

Many of the Yanks soon got invited to tea by the ladies and on the whole got on well with the local working-class people. The local children did very well with gifts of chewing gum, sweets and ice cream. Some of the ladies' fathers soon began to acquire packets of Camel cigarettes and other expensive brands. The American Motor Transport Company parked its lorries on the corporation tip in Mill Lane, alongside the Ford Brook. We lads, trainspotting at Ryecroft shed, soon investigated these strange-looking trucks. At the entrance to the tip were two armed guards both chewing gum. We enquired what manufacture the trucks were and we soon became familiar with Studebakers, Dodges, Chevrolets and GMCs. The Yanks on guard were quite astonished when we enquired what GMC stood for. One of them replied, 'Lads it stands for General Motor Corporation, the most powerful institution in North America and most of the world for that matter. It is in fact our God for its wealth is supreme and we shall eventually rule this world'. This remark probably began to make us believe in politics, for on our way home we discussed amongst ourselves whether we would be on the right side living with the Yankee dollar or under the jackboot of Hitler's Nazis or Stalin's Communists, despite fighting along with the former.

Situated at the junction of Lichfield Road and Mellish Road was a church hall beneath the church itself. This hall was full to capacity with GIs, like St Patrick's Hall. The Yanks would often be seen marching to the grammar school playing fields down Birmingham Road for training and PT exercises. Alan Price, while attending games as a grammar school pupil, remembers having Yankee cigarettes given to them when the teachers were out of sight and trying the well-known Camel brand. The smell and taste was most obnoxious to lads having their first smoke. They came to the conclusion that this cigarette was made from camel dung.

During the war that raged in the North African desert in 1941 to 1943, many Italian prisoners were captured. Many were shipped to England, including about 200 who were accommodated in Park Hall in Park Hall Lane, just off the main Birmingham Road. This area being somewhat upper class, it caused some consternation amongst local residents, but, owing to the fact that there was a war on, all protests about the visitors were in vain. What surprised the locals was the amount of freedom which they had, which was denied our servicemen in prison camps. On a summer evening, groups of them would be seen strolling along the lanes leading up to Barr Beacon in their brown-dyed uniforms with odd patches of various colours sown on haphazardly to make them easily identifiable. A considerable number of females chose to go long walks in this area when previously they would not.

These Italians were made to work on the railways, assisting the permanent way department. With the railways working to full capacity and carrying extra tonnage, these prisoners of war did a very useful job. One task I well remember them undertaking was to re-lay the old Midland Railway line from Ryecroft and Lichfield Road Junction to Wolverhampton. This line was only used for the occasional freight. Its passenger service had ceased in 1931. Its importance was for emergency use in case of enemy action involving the Grand Junction and Stour Valley lines that were used to almost saturation point between Birmingham and Wolverhampton.

To illustrate the excitement of living during the Second World War for us lads, I remember that, although we were working twelve hours a day for most of the week, we undertook cycle rides for some pleasure and to see what was happening away from Walsall. One Sunday afternoon ride took some of us first to Cannock. On the way we passed several pits all at work, with steam rising from the engine houses and the wheels on the winding gear spinning continuously as much-needed coal for industry was brought to the surface. After leaving Cannock we descended Shoal Hill, which was crowded with people relaxing in the sun and restoring their energy for the next week's slog. We crossed the mineral line from Littleton Colliery to the main line between Penkridge and Gailey as a train of empty wagons returned to the pit. We joined the main road to Wolverhampton at Penkridge. Just before war broke out this road was modified into a dual carriageway from before Gailey to the Wolverhampton boundary near Coven Heath, approximately five miles long. This was a venture which was to precede the expansion for the pending motor boom. What interested us was that we had special bicycle tracks to ride on. During the war the government decided to close the southbound road and used it for storage of army equipment consisting of army lorries, tanks, Bren gun carriers, field guns and anti-aircraft guns. Soldiers were billeted at regular intervals along this road and at certain points, blister hangars accommodating repair facilities were built across the road. Soldiers could be seen on guard with rifles and also in nearby fields machine-gun posts were situated, in case of enemy aircraft paying a visit. At the same time, while cycling along this temporary army ordnance camp, the sky above was never clear of aircraft. We then arrived in Wolverhampton at about 6.00 p.m. as workers were leaving work from the nearby Boulton and Paul aircraft works and the giant Goodyear tyre plant at Dunstall Park. Then back home to prepare for the next week's work. I was now about sixteen years old and I, along with other lads and girls, received notice to report to Walsall Labour Exchange for an interview for war work. We were encouraged to join either the navy, army or air force cadets to acclimatise us for the compulsory national call-up at eighteen. However in my case, as I was working more than ten hours a day maintaining Walsall's bus fleet, I was exempt.

In the spring of 1944 the activity in the Walsall area was enormous. A daily sight on the roads was the British and American Army convoys heading southwards, often exceeding one hundred or more trucks. Witnesses tell me of the gigantic American convoys along the Chester Road that, when approaching Shire Oak traffic lights, passed on nose to tail ignoring the red light despite at times the appearance of the law.

Around the beginning of June 1944 I was finishing a fortnight's holiday, which I had spent cycling as usual. Obviously I found myself at Lichfield Trent Valley station again. Trains were passing by almost as soon as each signalling section was clear. Otherwise the area and the old Burton Road Bridge were deserted. However at about midday some railway permanent way workers appeared and proceeded to demolish a wooden fence backing on to a small triangular field on the up side of the slow line that was used by local passenger trains. The gate leading to this small field from the old Burton Road near the Trent Valley top signal box and level crossing was also demolished. The men then departed. About one hour later I saw a most unusual sight, a Patriot class locomotive pulled into the up goods loop in the up reception sidings on the north side of the main Burton Road Bridge. A local passenger train on the Stafford to Rugby service pulled in the up platform and departed after an up express had cleared Hademore Crossing signal box. In the next half hour I was to witness railway and military planning at its best. The special train from the up goods loop slowly moved into Lichfield low-level up platform hauled by Patriot locomotive No. 5539 *E. C. Trench*. At the same time a convoy of American troop-carrying trucks arrived from nearby Whittington Army Barracks, full to capacity with GI soldiers complete with rifles and full kit. As they unloaded from their trucks they marched single file through the field then onto the platform to board the train. No time was lost and *E. C. Trench* pulled out of Lichfield low level immediately after an up express. Several up express trains passed the troop train whilst loading up its human cannon fodder for the imminent D-Day invasion of the Continent, and as it departed another troop train hauled by another Patriot No. 5534 *E. Tootle Broadhurst* steamed into the up platform. Meanwhile, on the Burton Old Road Bridge, congestion ruled supreme, with trucks and Yanks forming some sort of queue to enter. The revving up of trucks' engines as they strove to make a three-point turn in the narrow gateway, plus the orders and shouts from sergeants and officers as they tried to organise things, made a terrible din. The signalman in Trent Valley top box looked down on the proceedings in amazement, having been used to rural tranquillity. By about 8.00 p.m. when I left to cycle home about six more specials had departed, hauled by Stanier Black Five locomotives.

On my way home I decided to return to Trent Valley the following day. I set out early seeing as another hot summer day was promised and I decided to go via Tamworth. This was to pass Whittington Barracks but no British soldiers were in evidence. Instead, encamped in all the surrounding playing fields and parade grounds were literally thousands of American GIs milling about around bell tents. I arrived back at Trent Valley station at about midday to find it deserted, but at approximately 2.00 p.m. the convoys arrived again from Whittington Barracks to meet another succession of southbound troop trains which worked to the previous day's system. To this day I often wonder what happened to those American allies. These trains continued to move American soldiers until well after the D-Day landings.

On D-Day, 6 June, I was back at work at Birchills bus depot to witness the sight of hundreds of aeroplanes passing over Walsall for most of the day. The sky at times was full of Short Stirling, Handley Page Halifax, Armstrong Whitworth, Whitley and Douglas CD3 Dakotas, all towing Hengest and Horsa troop-carrying gliders. Soon, people were tuning into the radio which confirmed the invasion of France. Everyone was most excited and a spirit of friendliness existed in all walks of life. After the landings the

Yanks seemed to be arriving in vast numbers to replace those departed for France. The Sunday after D-Day I cycled to Sutton Park and Sutton Coldfield town which were full of Americans who had acquired accommodation in most of the large houses in the vicinity of the town centre. I remember a shop situated on the Parade which was converted into a Forces canteen and named 'The Doughnut Dugout'. As I passed by, jeeps and trucks were parked outside. If it was not for the passing Midland Red buses you could have imagined you were in a small-size American town. While sampling the American way of life I was accosted by three WACs with bicycles (these WACs were the American equivalent of our British ATS girls). They had evidently only just arrived in England and were billeted in some army huts situated in Streetly Lane, just inside Sutton Park. They asked me to show them some typical English villages. We set off for Shenstone and we gradually got to understand each other's language, their American drawl and my Black Country twang. The prettiness and cleanliness of Shenstone appealed to them and the small hedge-protected lanes around Weeford, Hints and Bassets Pole, with the tranquillity appertaining to this mode of life, greatly impressed these young girls, overseas for the first time. They asked to see Lichfield Cathedral, which we saw in the distance, but time did not allow this. In any case they soon became tired after riding strange bicycles, so we returned to their billets. The one problem I had with them was of their habit of riding on the right-hand side of the road, but, fortunately, with petrol rationing we virtually had the roads to ourselves. As I left them I was plied with chocolates and chewing gum and I left with a memory of a pleasant experience and with respect for the ordinary American citizens.

Back in Walsall people were now beginning to enjoy themselves as the war progressed in our favour and as the allies established a foothold in France. The biggest boom in entertainment was at the local cinemas which were playing to full audiences, with the sight of cinema queues after about 5.00 p.m. being a daily occurrence. In these queues almost every girl would be accompanied by a sailor, soldier, airman or Yank. The Town Hall dances would often have to refuse admission to their Saturday evening dance, such was the demand. Even small dance halls like the Masonic in Freer Street and local church halls would be so crowded that dancing was almost impossible. It was surprising by today's standards that on weekends whole families would be departing from Walsall by cycle. With money earned with wartime overtime, many married couples over calling-up age invested in tandems and most teenagers owned a decent cycle. My neighbours, the Taylor family of 76 Webster Rd, had seven daughters of whom two, Betty and Mary Taylor, were keen on cycling. With other girls, we spent the last two war years cycling. About three months after D-Day some of us decided to ride to Milford via Rugeley. Going through Hednesford we passed hundreds of air force personnel in the town from the nearby aerodrome near Brindley Heath. As we descended down the incline to Rugeley, we stopped to watch a football match between England and Germany, for right adjacent to the main road was a hastily erected prisoner of war camp housing about 5,000 Germans. It was very heavily guarded with large barbed-wire fences and sentry towers with soldiers manning machine guns. We stopped and watched this match between our soldiers and the prisoners who seemed to be enjoying cordial relations. We cycled on to Milford to find the common and hillside packed with people and literally hundreds of cycles. Very few motor cars were in evidence but extra Midland Red buses were running on the Stafford to Rugeley service. I believe that at this late stage of the war, bus undertakings were allowed extra allowances for pleasure trips to give war workers some means of escape from the long hours spent in industry. The Yanks were also very much in evidence at Milford, for a military hospital had been set up in the grounds of Shugborough Hall and several hundred wounded GIs could be seen taking their first steps on the road to recovery. I did wonder at the time if some of them were those GIs that I had watched filling troop trains at Lichfield Trent Valley station a few weeks previously.

Another Sunday cycle ride as the war was drawing to a close involved a trip to Trentham Gardens near Stoke-on-Trent. As Betty Taylor and myself rode across Cannock Chase and through Stafford we encountered more cyclists than ever. In fact, they outnumbered motors, which made cycling a pleasure instead of today's constant harassment by the motoring fraternity. On arrival at Trentham Gardens, the crowds were enormous, with a regular shuttle of Potteries buses bringing people from the five main towns of the Potteries' conurbation. Bicycles were stacked in their thousands near the entrance and were left in safety without padlocks, while people enjoyed the freedom of Trentham Gardens. We rode back in the evening, passing numerous tandems with a perspiring male at the front. It was on this ride that we came to the conclusion that the Second World War was almost at its climax. Looking back to 1940 and 1941 no one was enjoying themselves as on this 1944 summer day.

The news from the war fronts was of continued success through to Christmas 1944 and it came as no surprise that on 8 May 1945 the war ended in Europe. From what I remember we heard the news whilst at work and it soon got around that the following day was to be a general bank holiday. On the same evening it seemed that most of Walsall's citizens had decided to walk to the town centre. All transport ceased to run and by the time some of the Webster Road boys and girls arrived on The Bridge we found the crowds had grown to such proportions that Park Street, Bridge Street and the area about St Paul's church and the bus station were full of people singing and dancing and, in general, making merry. The local public houses stayed open, however, and to my knowledge there was no shortage of beer. Amongst all this jollification there was no trouble or vandalism. The pleasant surprise was that most shops and buildings allowed their lights to blaze. After almost six years of blackout, to see Walsall lit up again was a relief. The following day almost every street arranged a party and in no time streets and houses became festooned with streamers and decorations. Somehow the womenfolk contrived to make sandwiches, jellies and ice creams despite being still on ration. Dancing, singing and games went on until after midnight, leaving many children to be put to bed exhausted with their clothes still on. Likewise many adults finished the day in a state of intoxication. One resident of Webster Road, who earned a living as a bus driver, got somewhat carried away by the festivities. With Birchills bus depot being completely void of any staff, he decided to borrow a double-decker bus and take a number of local children over Cannock Chase for a free ride. Unfortunately a few days after VE Day he was called to see the general manager, who promptly gave him the sack. The next event that followed VE Day was the dropping of the atomic bomb on Japan which finally put an end to the Second World War. More festivities and street parties took place again in Walsall with another bank holiday and from then Walsall reverted back to peace-time living that, happily, has continued to the present day. In Walsall's case the war did one good thing, it saw the end of the insecurity of unemployment and poor living standards of the 1920s and 1930s that the working class had had to endure.

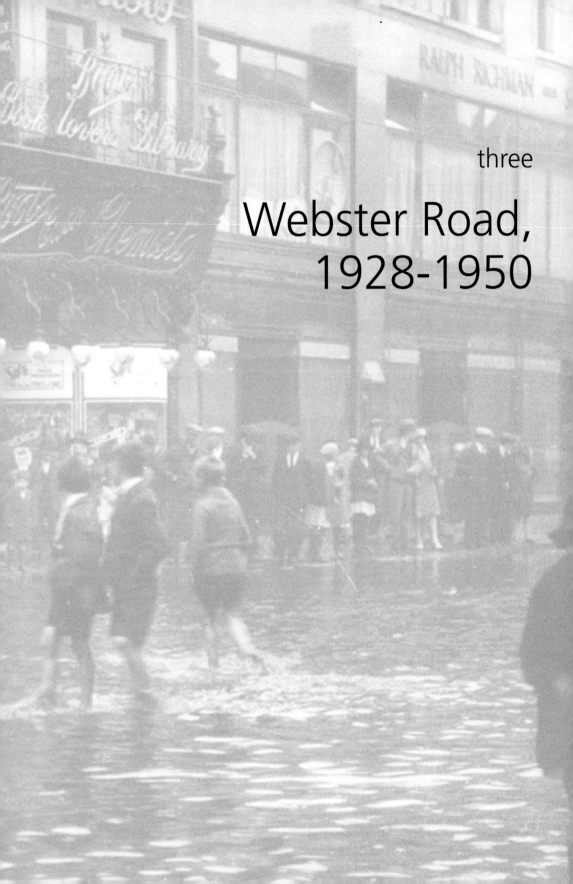

three

Webster Road, 1928-1950

After leaving the army in 1918, after four years serving with the Royal Garrison Artillery in France, my father was, like many of his compatriots, seeking work in a land fit for heroes to live in. His aim in life was simple: he wanted a regular job, then to get married and acquire a house of his own. After army service he lived at No. 10 Hospital Street. Eventually he managed to secure employment at Birchills tram depot by sheer persistence. He stood outside the office of the general manager of Walsall Corporation Trams each morning and enquired about the possibility of employment. He knew full well the merits of working for the corporation. It was a job for life, providing one was punctual and reliable. His ploy eventually paid off and he was offered a job cleaning tramcars on permanent night duty from 10.00 p.m. until 6.00 a.m. for six days a week. He had met my mother, Miss Florrie Keeling of 47 Long Street, before being sent to France in 1914. He got married in 1924 but still lived with his mother at 10 Hospital Street. An application was forwarded to Walsall Housing Committee for one of the new council houses being built with government aid to relieve unemployment. To qualify for a house one must have children and that is why I, Jack Haddock, came into the world on 17 September 1927.

During this year a firm of building contractors, from Scunthorpe I think, won a contract to erect some houses to the north of Essex Street. Forest Lane was widened for houses to be erected on the south side. A new road from Forest Lane was to run parallel with Essex Street and, when built, was to be named Suffolk Street with a small street branching off to be called Rutland Street. At about this time Walsall honoured one of its citizens, Flight-Lieutenant Webster, who, in 1927, won the Schneider Trophy breaking the air-speed record in doing so. The town council decided to name the proposed Suffolk Street, Webster Road instead. My father, working at Birchills tram depot, wanted to reside as near as possible to work. This was commonplace thinking among working men between the wars. One could reach work easily, especially in inclement weather, and with no travel costs.

With new council houses about to be built in the North Walsall area, my father put in a written request to rent a council house to the Walsall housing manager, Mr Bywater. The interview was duly granted and at a precise date and time he attended. From previous applicants for housing my father took the advice to be well dressed and clean shaven and to wear a collar and tie. After army life this was no problem to him but he recalled that the interview was almost an interrogation, with constant probes into his personal life, particularly as to whether or not he had ever been involved with the law. The council of those days would only cater for law-abiding citizens and respectable people. After an interview of almost one hour, the housing manager said he could grant my father a house in Webster Road on condition that he would submit three references from prominent people in authority. My father wrote to the Royal Artillery Headquarters, which duly obliged with an exemplary reference for his four years serving in France. The general manager of Walsall Corporation Transport also gave an excellent reference. Finally my father approached a local JP, Mr McShane, who lived in North Walsall, who supplied a good reference willingly. One day in late Summer 1928 a letter arrived from the housing department telling my father to call and collect the key for 78 Webster Road. As father was at work, mother lost no time in collecting the key (in those days a man would not leave his place of employment even for such an important occasion). Father inspected the house the very same evening and immediately instructed mother to call as soon as possible in the morning and accept the conditions of the tenancy.

Webster Road, 1981. In 1927 contractors from Scunthorpe won the contract to build houses north of the existing Kent and Essex Streets. At first the road was to be called Suffolk Street. However, the name was changed to Webster Road in honour of the Walsall man, Flight-Lieutenant Webster, who won the Schneider Trophy, setting a new air-speed record in 1927.

Despite the harsh economic climate of the time our family and all the new residents of Webster Road found themselves living in paradise after the trials and tribulations of the previous war and the early twenties. Living with our new neighbours was a very pleasant experience. The socialist spirit amongst the new settlers was second to none. Everyone was willing to help the other with tasks like building garden sheds and digging up the old farmland for gardens. The bulk of the new residents were either railwaymen from Ryecroft shed, tram and bus staff from Birchills depot or some local Co-op men. Others were factory workers and council office staff. Within six months of Webster Road being full of residents, every garden had been cultivated for growing vegetables at the rear of the houses, front gardens were lined with privet hedges and lawns were laid with surrounding flower beds. Because of limited financial resources, various expedients were used to save money. To save purchasing expensive grass seed, the locals set out with a wheelbarrow to the meadows alongside a small brook running parallel between the present-day Dartmouth Avenue and Holdens Crescent, long before the houses were built. Cuttings about two square feet were taken from selected, weed-free parts of the meadows. These cuttings formed the basis of many Webster Road lawns that still exist today.

The housewives of Webster Road were proud of their new abodes. On washing days it was a regular feature to wash paths and outside footpaths with leftover soap suds. No stray dogs were to be seen roaming the street. The real dog-lovers would keep their animals chained up in their own back gardens and take them for exercise on a lead, only releasing them on nearby fields. Friendships developed, though of a formal nature. The children soon developed a system of games that was played for hours on nearby Gilbert's

Top: *Tram on The Bridge, early 1920s. The first tramways in Walsall opened in December 1884. They were electrified in 1893. The corporation purchased the lines within the borough from 1 January 1901. From about the end of 1901 all services operated from a terminal on The Bridge.*

Above: *Buses on The Bridge, c. 1930. The Walsall Corporation Act of 1914 included powers to operate motor buses on specified routes. The first motor bus service opened in 1915. By 1930 the corporation was using trams and more motor buses. The bus stop for Sutton Road and Birmingham Road buses was on The Bridge.*

farmland or the sand hole situated at the top end of Webster Road. This disused sand pit was owned by the corporation, after being given to them in the will of Mr C.C. Walker, otherwise known as 'Coddy'. Coddy Walker was Mayor of Walsall several times and when his sand pit was in operation he would not hesitate to call the police to any children playing in his sand. It surprised everyone in Walsall therefore when he gave this land to the children of North Walsall and Ryecroft, with instructions for swings and slides to be erected. In 1936 the corporation decided to fill in this sand hole with household refuse, causing an epidemic of scarlet fever and diphtheria amongst local children. Millions of flies caused much sickness during the hot summer of 1936. It was not until 1966 that the sand hole was landscaped and the swings were erected in 1970.

In the 1930s motor cars were few and far between in Webster Road. Horse-drawn milk and bread carts could be seen during the mornings. The Walsall Co-op Society had most of the customers in Webster Road because of its dividend system. The Co-op baker and milkman were most respected by the Webster Road citizens. They were always smartly dressed and well mannered. I very much doubt if the spirit and comradeship of those pre-Second World War local Co-op, bus and railwaymen will ever be seen again. Some private milkmen and bakers, who were also very friendly, traded with people in the old terraced houses of Walsall who had been customers for decades. They were also respected, obliging and well-liked. I well remember the baker's two-wheeled, covered bread carts with the name of Scribbans and Hooper and the milk drays of Gouldens and the Co-op. These vendors and deliverymen would always arrive at a set time and would be regular and never have a day off.

The corporation housing repair men were always very popular with the residents. Although the houses were relatively new, maintenance was still necessary. In the 1930s, if a tenant required a job done, a complaint was made to the rent man, who called weekly, (the rent was approximately seven shillings). The rent man examined the problem, made a decision and notified Hollemeadow Avenue Housing Repairs. The following day workmen would arrive to carry out repairs; this was the system in those days. These workmen would arrive pushing a two-wheel handcart with their tools. I have seen them pushing one of these handcarts loaded with housebricks, sand and cement. Every few years the council would come around to decorate one upstairs and one downstairs room. In the case of the North Walsall area the council erected a wooden hut at the side of No. 101 Webster Road to be used as a base for these activities instead of walking from Hollemeadow Avenue. The handcart and hut were never vandalised. Each morning the two council decorators set off with their handcart loaded with ladders, planks and paint. Young children would often be given a free ride by these very reliable and popular council workers. In those days all the Webster Road council houses were coal-fired. Thus at most times of each day coalmen would be in evidence with their horse-drawn coal carts that used to carry their own scales. Coal was about two shillings and sixpence a hundredweight. If the coalman spilled any coal on the road or path he would sweep it up and give it to the householder. One feature of all this horse traffic was the abundance of horse manure, but, as everyone cultivated their gardens, there was fierce competition for the droppings. Collecting this manure was a lucrative way for local children to earn pocket money. Sometimes they were paid the princely sum of three pence a bucket or sixpence for a barrowful.

Most of the new residents of Webster Road had children. They all attended North Walsall School. Firm friendships soon developed, resulting in well-organised games taking place on the nearby sand hole and in the street. As dusk fell some games were

Sam Kimberley's shop, corner of Hospital Street and Gladstone Street, 1958. The site is now occupied by Gladstone House old people's home. Hospital Street was renamed after the epidemic hospital opened here in 1872. People refused to use the hospital during the smallpox epidemic of 1875 until Sister Dora took charge.

played under the street gas lamps, but on the odd occasion the residents would object to excessive noise or to trampling on the newly formed front gardens which were ideal for hide and seek. By about 1933 almost every house in Webster Road boasted a well-dressed privet hedge and trim front lawn. Any problems with the children were dealt with by their respective parents. At no time were the police called, in fact police were a rarity around this part of North Walsall. The occasional foot patrol put in the odd appearance, but would be seen more often or not in Ryecroft where the occasional misdemeanours occurred. With high unemployment during the Depression, the favourite crime was coal pinching. The Ryecroft engine sheds were the prime target. A foggy night was welcomed by the 'Ryecroft gang' for these nocturnal, illegal activities, but the popular means of procuring coal took place on the Cannock line railway cutting to the northern side of Webster Road. Until 1939 there was no housing on the site of today's Beddows Road; it was then farmland belonging to Farmer Gilbert. The recognised system was to jump on the slow-moving coal trains descending from Bloxwich that, owing to the severe gradient, did not exceed walking pace. Many tons were lost by the LMS railway during the Depression because of illegal sales around Ryecroft. A number of local Ryecroft men eventually had to spend their holidays at a rather spartan Birmingham hotel known as Winson Green for their trouble.

A number of us enterprising kids of Webster Road used to visit a local tip in Mill Lane situated beside the Ford Brook, known as the 'Fleam'. This tip was a source of old pram axles and timber. In no time we all possessed our own barrows and by scrounging paint had our names painted on the side of our proud contraptions. The juvenile haulage contractors found plenty of work from the new Webster Road tenants as they improved their gardens. Most of the inhabitants had never had the opportunity to possess a garden after living in the old-fashioned terraced houses with communal backyards with shared washhouses and toilets. Most new citizens of Webster Road decided to lay a pathway down the garden. With the men at work during the day it was up to the lads to provide commodities like cement and sand for their needs. Sand was in abundance from the disused sand hole at the top of Webster Road. Thus for sixpence a barrow some of us lads would have a number of deliveries each week. Some of the residents were pigeon fanciers, who would each have his regular lad, who, during school holidays, would earn extra cash for cleaning out the pigeon pens and disposing of the used sand and droppings on the Mill Lane tip. The hardest job for us lads was to convey large quantities of housebricks. We travelled miles about town to where old houses were being demolished, but for a heavy load of dressed bricks we would probably be paid nine pence – a small fortune in those days. When some of the residents decided to lay a concrete path, we made regular trips with our barrows to Moseleys, the building contractors and coal wharf next to Birchills bus depot. The price of a bag of cement was three shillings and sixpence. By 1936 Webster Road was beginning to look a splendid sight with its tidy gardens and clean streets.

The 1930s period of Webster Road saw a succession of hot summers. The tar on the road melted quite often. This obviously attracted children, who dipped wood in the molten tar and then proceeded to paint various names on the pavement. However, our friend the rent man took a dim view of this practice and our parents made us scrape the tar off when solid. Every few years the road was re-laid with new granite chippings. This meant a visit by one of the corporation steam rollers. Often, while the men were having a break for 'snap', any mothers who had children with whooping cough (this complaint was commonplace in those days), would produce a well washed out jam jar to be filled with hot tar from the tar boiler. The afflicted children were made to sniff the tar until cold. I am led to believe this remedy was, within reason, successful. Another attraction was the horse-drawn water cart during a heat wave. The children spent hours following the cart and running in the cool water. At the same time they chanted to the driver as he progressed at a leisurely walking pace: 'The corporation water cart was full up to the brim, the corporation driver fell in and could not swim, he sank right to the bottom just like a little stone and all the little fishes sang, there's no place like home.' This was a fine example of North Walsall School poetry.

One late evening towards the end of September 1933, there was an event that almost every citizen in Webster Road attended. It was to see the last tramcar from Walsall to Bloxwich. From about 10.30 p.m. residents began the trek to Bloxwich Road via Forest Lane. Most of the residents as usual left their houses unlocked. Each local street turned out to witness the end of a way of life, and subsequently the Bloxwich Road saw a crowd like that of a football match. The same conditions applied for the three miles from Walsall to Bloxwich. The last tram finally passed to tremendous cheers and hand claps with its tram bell ringing continually. Going back down Webster Road it was like a seafront parade with fathers carrying young ones already in slumber in their arms.

The gas and electricity meter men visited every three months and each time my mother made good use of the rebate to balance the family budget. The coin for the gas meter was one penny and for the electric sixpence or one shilling. The poor old gasman would be seen towards the end of the morning or afternoon sweating with his large leather bag of heavy coins making his way to pay the money in at the Town Hall.

Now I will try to remember two of our first neighbours, along with exchanges up to the Second World War, their employment and upbringing and also their children and how they progressed in life. No. 40 Webster Road was an attraction for us lads. Mr Freeman who resided there reared a family of three lads, Albert, John and Peter and a daughter. Mr Freeman drove one of the first petrol lorries around Walsall for the Shell-Mex Company and used to come home to dinner with the lorry. It was always parked outside the house when we children returned to afternoon school. It was an Albion type and one could smell the petrol as we passed by. The Freemans were always involved in motor transport as the years progressed and in the 1970s Albert owned his own motor coach

Walsall's last tram, 30 September 1933. The Bloxwich tram route was the last Walsall tram route to close. It was replaced by trolleybuses the next day. The corporation had promoted the Walsall Corporation Act 1925 to allow it to use trolleybuses. The first trolleybus service opened in 1931 to Willenhall.

firm. At No. 77 lived Mr Bill Bate, his wife, and daughter, Joyce. Bill was a railwayman for fifty years in the service of the LNWR and LMS and retired in the early days of British Rail. In 1913 he had the honour of being one of the first three bus drivers when the LNWR operated the first bus services across southern Cannock Chase from Brownhills. This was prior to Walsall Corporation running a bus service, but the First World War interfered with this experimental bus service. After hostilities ceased, Walsall Corporation ran the Chase bus services and Bill Bate finished the rest of his working days on the footplate as fireman and driver, after serving in France as an ambulance driver in the Royal Army Medical Corps (RAMC). Bill was a very good photographer prior to the Second World War and possessed both Leica and Rollicord cameras. He was a very clever man, capable of making his own furniture and other household requirements and, like most railwaymen, was the owner of an immaculate garden.

Despite the harsh economic climate of the 1930s, my father somehow managed to take mother and myself on a week's holiday to Blackpool in the summer of 1937. He had acquired the money by working overtime during the previous bad winter. He was classed as a handyman at Birchills bus depot. One of his overtime jobs was working on the trolleybus overhead wiring during Saturday nights, until midday Sunday. This was the most convenient time to erect long sections of new wiring and it was most lucrative financially. Many nights he was called about midnight during heavy snowfalls to fit skid chains to the motor buses that had to cope with the exposed Cannock Chase routes. He had made his mind up to go to Blackpool with this extra cash, as his last visit to Blackpool had been on his honeymoon after leaving the army, after the First World War. The big day finally arrived and we set off from platform 2 on Walsall station on a special excursion. The train was made up of vintage LNWR rolling stock and for the whole of the trip I was rushing from one side of the compartment to the other trying to spot as many engines as possible. Looking back I must have been quite a pest to our fellow passengers.

We arrived at Blackpool North station and I found myself in another world. The first thing I noticed as we walked down Talbot Road was the smell. Not an obnoxious smell, but one different from Walsall's leather factories and industrial smells, one of the aroma of fish and chip shops mingling with the smell of dry sand blown from the beach. We duly reported to our digs and were given a dinner of fish and chips. The next week's holiday convinced me that all northern people lived solely on this diet. My meal was eaten in record time in my anxiety to see the sea for the first time. We reached Talbot Square and I shall never forget the first sight of the sea that looked rather dirty to me, instead of the image I had acquired of sea being deep blue. The sounds of the screaming seagulls and tooting horns of the Blackpool trams gave me a feeling of being in a new age. I had never seen so many people before – they reminded me of a swarm of ants. They did, however, all seem to be laughing, smiling and enjoying themselves. I was impressed by the Lancashire accent but at first could not understand it. Our digs overlooked Blackpool North station excursion platforms and the sight of the morning arrivals disgorging many thousands of day trippers made me wonder how the railway managed to move so many people. The same applied to the exodus after teatime.

A visit to the Blackpool Tower was soon on the agenda, with my first visit to the top of the tower in the large claustrophobic lift. The view was marvellous, but the thing that really thrilled me was the sight of the De Havilland twin-engine aeroplanes circling the tower with novelty flights from Squires Gate Aerodrome. Hours were spent in the tower ballroom listening to Reginald Dixon on the famous tower organ and the dance orchestra of Bertini. A visit to the Winter Gardens was made, to visit the cinema to see a film on current release with Shirley Temple singing the hit song 'On the Good Ship Lollipop'.

We made a trip to Fleetwood one afternoon – my first ride on one of Blackpool's streamlined tramcars. We met some friends who were going to the Isle of Man. We saw them off to board the Manx steamer *Lady of Man*. I well remember an old lady departing with a large crowd of what must have been theatrical people, all singing 'Has Anyone Here Seen Kelly, Kelly from the Isle of Man'. We were informed by interested onlookers that the lady was the great Florrie Ford of music hall fame. The boat departed with its siren hooting, in contrast to the screaming cries of the seagulls. Also, as it must have been about high tide, a number of Fleetwood's trawlers began to arrive with their decks well loaded and oilskin figures anxiously awaiting a visit home. Back in Blackpool the rest of our time was spent at the Pleasure Beach, Madame Tussaud's Waxworks and the Tower Circus. Thus ended my first week away from Walsall.

One occasion I well remember, about 1937, was a visit to the Grand Theatre. We had booked our tickets some days previously. During the day heavy snow fell and by the time we set out for the show the snow was approximately one foot high. The trolleybus we boarded was in trouble all the way to town, skidding and sliding through drifts. We finally made it to the Grand and as we awaited the curtain call we were not surprised to see only about twenty people in the stalls and gallery. I cannot recall the main attraction of the bill that night, but my father was very impressed by a young comedian who was way down in the bill. He told me on the way back home, as we struggled through the still falling snow, that this chap had got style and had the makings of a famous star. All I remember of him was that he spoke that fast I could not hear his jokes and that he possessed the largest mouth I had ever seen. Many years later I found out that Dad was right, for the gentleman concerned was none other than Tommy Trinder.

My grandma lived at No. 10 Hospital Street. She had a very kind nature and was always helping people. She ran a club for poor people in the Stafford Street and Ryecroft districts for a local cobbler, a Mr Harry Downs of 111 Stafford Street. She used to take me on her visits to these people and I most vividly recall going into Ryecroft Street and Ryecroft Park. Here there was great poverty. The houses must have been the worst slums in Walsall with the possible exception of Peal Street and the streets around St Matthew's church, where the upper classes worshipped without any thought for the inhabitants of the area.

Ryecroft Street and Ryecroft Park were near to St Peter's church and a similar situation prevailed. My grandma, Mrs Brough, used to take me to Ryecroft Street, which was better known as Pig Sty Park. She used to buy shoes from Harry Downs for the down and outs there, to be paid back weekly, a few pence at a time. The houses they lived in had no back doors. To go to the communal lavatory and washhouse one had to go via the entry. The lavatories were of the old-fashioned 'mix-ins' type, with used ashes emptied by the night soil man. In summer the smell was revolting, with the usual swarm of flies. The street was used by most inhabitants to empty their teapots. All the tea leaves and horse manure only added to the aroma. The only time Pig Sty Park smelled reasonably clean was after a very heavy thunderstorm or a long period of heavy rain. Not a blade of grass or plant life grew here. The locals used to joke that the only tree in Pig Sty Park was the tumbledown public house known as the 'Yew Tree'. I remember gran taking me into one house – only a battered old table covered with newspapers stood out. On it was a sugar bag, teapot and jam jars for drinking out of, plus some unwashed plates with egg stains congealed solid, along with a few empty beer and stout bottles. The man in residence was lying on a sofa

Pig in the street, Ryecroft, 1930s. It is not known where the animal had come from. Pig clubs were a common feature during the Second World War. Prior to this the animals were kept locally in yards or on open ground. There were men who were skilled in slaughtering who were called in when a pig was ready for butchering.

with all the upholstery removed and wooden planks nailed to the frame. To the rear of Ryecroft Park was Moulds Foundry with its cupola belching flame and depositing its dust and fumes on these unfortunate inhabitants, living behind the relatively prosperous Stafford Street.

In 1936 my father's half brother, my Uncle George, was working for the well-known Birmingham firm of Fisher & Ludlow. His job qualified him for a company car, a rare distinction in those days. The car was a Morris 12hp saloon. He used to take our family on regular outings. At weekends I used to stay in one of the firm's houses in Rae Street, with a backyard view of the foul-smelling River Rae.

Uncle George and father used to spend most of their time in a public house in the vicinity of Bradford Street called The Spotted Dog. They used to take me along with them while mother and auntie did shopping in Birmingham. I was left to sit on the pub steps, with a bottle of pop and crisps. This was the usual solace of beer drinking parents to their children. It suited me, however, for I was in the fresh air and was occupied with collecting tram numbers off the constant procession of trams along Bradford Street, along with the corporation and Midland Red buses that passed every few minutes. I was happy to just watch this transport scene and could not understand why men chose to spend hours in a public house drinking beer and visiting the toilet along with smoking and creating a foul atmosphere, instead of being outside in the sunlight. One day uncle had the offer of a new council house at Acocks Green and we all helped him to move from Rae Street. The new house was in Severne Road, part of a new, large estate similar to the London Metroland. It was a very pleasant environment, all the houses having privet hedges and

Bradford Place, 1930. Lord Jellicoe is laying a wreath at the cenotaph. Bradford Place and Bradford Street were named after the Earl of Bradford, who was a major landowner and lord of the manor of Walsall. Other streets in the town also commemorate the family. The cenotaph was unveiled in 1921 in honour of Walsall men who died in the First World War.

well-kept gardens. Many weekends were spent at No. 107 Severne Road, with trips in the car.

One trip that stands out in my memory is a visit to Castle Bromwich Aerodrome to a Royal Air Force flying display. Most of the aircraft performing aerobatics were Gloster Gladiators, Hawker Demons and Bristol Biplanes. On the airfield there were some new monoplanes on display. Looking back with hindsight I must have been viewing some of the Spitfire and Hurricane prototypes. Of the larger aircraft there was a number of bombers consisting of Handley Page Harrows, Hendons and the latest Hampdens, also Bristol Bombays and Vickers Virginias. This collection of fighting aircraft was then our front line of defence, which makes me wonder how we survived the first years of the Second World War. The crowds witnessing this air display were large despite the Depression. Most of them came by train to nearby Castle Bromwich station. Also a constant stream of Birmingham Corporation buses arrived to deposit more sightseers.

Another interesting trip in uncle's car was a visit to relations living in Bolton, Lancashire. It was a hot, summer's day and the car was fitted with a sliding roof. Going through the Potteries along the A34 we passed a number of smoking kilns, all belching white smoke. My father explained to me that this was the White Country in contrast to our Black Country. Passing into Manchester we halted at a swing bridge on the Manchester Ship Canal. I was amazed to see a large ship pass by; it was my first sight of a sea-going vessel. The largest I had previously seen was a canal boat.

Our relatives kept a small general stores on a road leading to Farnworth. Nearby was a very busy railway station known as 'Moses Gate'. I spent hours on the platform collecting the numbers of engines that did not appear in the Midlands, while my parents and relatives paid their usual visits to public houses. I was taken to a number of snooker halls in Bolton. One hall we visited was of considerable length, accommodating about twenty tables. With every player smoking I could not see the tables at one end for smoke and was always glad to get outside. One thing I recall about Bolton was the friendship and happiness of the Lancashire folk.

Town centre under flood, 1930s. This may have been the flood of 14 June 1931. Two inches of rain fell in forty-five minutes. In Lower Rushall Street Mrs Lawrence, who kept a grocery and general shop, had to retreat upstairs when her shop and house were flooded.

Flood in Park Street, 14 June 1931. An exceptional downpour on a Sunday caused cellars to flood but there was little damage to shop stock as, forewarned by previous events, most shopkeepers did not keep stock in their cellars. One manager arrived in time to place in position a special storm-water guard which he had made.

New George Hotel, The Bridge, post-1935. The George Hotel was opened by Thomas Fletcher in 1781. It stood on The Bridge at the corner of Digbeth. It was demolished and rebuilt between 1933 and 1935 and demolished again in 1979.

I had another uncle on my mother's side who made my life exciting. His name was Harry Poyner and he worked as a fireman at Ryecroft shed. One day in 1938 he gained promotion to Bushbury shed at Wolverhampton. A new housing estate was in the process of development in the Bushbury district. He acquired a house in Sherbourne Road – No. 38. It was another clean, pleasant community to live in, similar to Uncle George's area of Acocks Green. Many evening walks in summer were undertaken: the most popular was to walk along Three Tuns Lane into Marsh Lane with its hedgerows and wildlife, but it was about to become the victim of urban expansion. Bushbury Hill was a nice place then with a very pleasant view north, with miles of trees and hedges; today more houses have ruined the view. However Bushbury shed was the main attraction. One day I was taken down to the shed on uncle's pay day. Bushbury shed had the honour of providing most locomotives for the London-Wolverhampton service, which ran in competition with the GWR. Bushbury had just been allocated new Patriot class locomotives, also known as Baby Scots. Two were on show this particular day – No. 5521 *Ryhl* and No. 5532 *Illustrious*. These locomotives were spotlessly clean with the maroon paintwork glistening in the sunlight. Also on shed were two time-expired 'Prince of Wales' class locomotives, *Caliban* and *Kestral*, along with a crimson Midland Compound. The smell of steam and smoke was to me most exhilarating. The men working in the shed were happy and cheerful and life seemed pleasant around Bushbury. A bus service from Wolverhampton to Bushbury church was expanded to cater for the newcomers. The new Daimler COG 5 buses with Brush bodywork and green livery passed over Bushbury Bridge every few minutes, adding to the attraction of the passing trains.

Most of our trips to Bushbury were by cycle. It was a very pleasant ride. After trainspotting for the day us lads would call at auntie's house for some refreshment. We started our trip back home by climbing the steep sandy lane with sharp curves and high hedges on both sides. One had to stand on the pedals to climb this gradient, for it was a point of honour not to dismount and push the cycle up. There was always a trolleybus standing at the top of the hill as we made our way along Old Fallings Lane into Primrose Lane then across the Cannock Road into Blackhalve Lane. The trolleybuses that ran along the Cannock Road were the Sunbeam MS 2 models. Just inside Blackhalve Lane was a farmhouse that always had the attraction of a number of traction engines with farmyard equipment. They were in very good condition and must have been in use on local farms. As we progressed along Blackhalve Lane we came to the first of three level crossings on the mineral line from Hilton Colliery to Holly Bank Colliery. As the train approached the unguarded crossing a man jumped off the engine and stopped any road traffic with a red flag then allowed the train to cross. In most cases road traffic was non-existent. We often tried to get a ride on the train but all efforts were unsuccessful. As we cycled out of Blackhalve Lane into High Hill we used to venture down a cart track to see a coalmine complete with winding gear. It had not long ceased operation as the pit shaft had been covered with a steel plate. It made us wonder how men worked in such conditions. We then came into Upper Sneyd Road with its long row of miners' houses. In summer many retired miners sat about in groups passing the time away. They always waved or spoke to us lads and seemed interested in our trainspotting activities, and they all advised us not to go down the mines when we left school. We passed on down Sneyd Lane over the last of the colliery level crossings and into Bloxwich, then home. On all these cycle rides to Bushbury we always enjoyed ourselves and were never known to fall out with one another.

Old houses, George Street, 1956. In 1958 there was some residential property in George Street but much of the property was commercial. Occupants included a milliner, a café, army and navy suppliers, a firm undertaking building repairs and Shannons, the clothing manufacturers. Shannons' building is still there but many of the other buildings have now gone.

Construction of new Overstrand Café in High Street, 1960s. This shows the half-built café and how it changed the view looking up the High Street towards St Matthew's church. The café was part of a development by local traders operating as Digbeth (Walsall) Development Ltd.

four

North Walsall
School Holidays,
Summer 1937

The following account describes a typical day of self-made entertainment enjoyed by myself and my friends from the North Walsall area during the school holidays and at weekends. That we could enjoy the holiday hobby of trainspotting was thanks to our parents who, despite the unemployment and low wages of the times, somehow found the much-needed cash to provide us with bicycles. In 1937 it was possible for ten-year-old boys like ourselves to cycle safely to Lichfield, Birmingham and Wolverhampton for a whole day's trainspotting. At the same time we were also able to see tramcars, buses and canal boats. This is a recollection of one such ride to Lichfield Trent Valley station.

The object of this cycle ride to Lichfield was to collect the locomotive names and numbers of the new LMS-type engines and the various LNWR veterans then still operating. Those distant days, as seen by us ten year old lads, seemed very happy ones. The implications of certain events in Germany concerning Adolf Hitler did not register in our thoughts: in those days the sun always seemed to be shining. When not in school, most North Walsall lads spent their time on the Mill Lane bridges or in the field at the bottom of Brewer Street. During these gatherings, plans for trips to other regions were made, so that we could spot locomotives which were not normally to be seen in Walsall.

The year 1937 saw the coronation of King George VI and Queen Elizabeth. In celebration the LMS had inaugurated the famous *Coronation Scot*, a stream-lined train with blue and silver stripes running along its entire length. The thought of spotting this attraction was the reason for our extra trips to Lichfield during 1937.

It was on one of those halcyon summer days that a group of us North Walsall junior school lads, together with some other lads from the grammar school and Elmore Green School, set off. Starting from North Walsall junior school, we went via the Ryecroft sheds, where we stopped to look at the engines there, then on towards Lichfield for our

North Walsall infants school, 1933. Jack Haddock and Eve Dutton are standing at the rear of the photograph. North Walsall School, Derby Street, started as a council senior, junior and infants school in 1904. The senior department was recognized as a higher elementary school in 1906. It became a senior school for boys in 1929, a secondary modern after 1944 and closed in 1965.

Rushall Square, 1930s. The Square has always been the centre and focal point of Rushall. Before it was taken over by traffic it boasted a clock and drinking fountain with trough set up to commemorate Queen Victoria's jubilee. The fountain was made by the Coalbrookdale Company and the clock by Sheppard Brothers of Walsall.

day's entertainment. Our parents provided us with enough sandwiches, cake, apples and bottles of pop to sustain us through the day, but we had little money, perhaps just a few pennies. We started from Ryecroft at approximately 10.30 a.m., after waiting for the so-called '10.30 a.m. namer'. This was a local passenger train from Birmingham New Street going through to Crewe. It started first from Crewe in the early hours of the morning as a local train to Birmingham via Wolverhampton and the Stour Valley line, to return via Walsall and Rugeley Trent Valley. It was a train used as a 'running in-turn' for recently out-shopped main line locomotives. We observed it this particular morning hauled by the Royal Scot class No. 6155. The *Lancer* was making very easy work of its light load of three non-corridor coaches. As this train disappeared into Ryecroft cutting, the trip to Lichfield commenced. We joined the Lichfield Road and before passing under the Navvies Bridge (which in those days had a large advertisement for 'Worthington Ales' above its archway), we saw that passing above us on a Walsall-Birmingham local via Sutton Park was Ryecroft Fowler tank loco No. 17. The fireman waved to us lads. We proceeded uphill to Rushall and passed the county police station opposite the George and Dragon public house. A police constable was usually in evidence, so we were on our best behaviour at this point, because if you were caught fooling about on bikes or riding three abreast, say, you were in real trouble in those days. We passed across Rushall Square with its clock and water trough. On the old Labour Club building which was situated between the Lichfield Road and Pelsall Lane was a headboard which stated 'This site earmarked for a cinema'. This was the boom period for the cinema industry. We were pleased to think that we would have the choice of another cinema to go to in the near future, but Mr Adolf Hitler's intrusion into our way of life would soon dash all hopes of a cinema for Rushall. As we passed Rushall, we were overtaken by a Walsall Corporation blue bus, No. 8, operating on the No. 23 route, Walsall to Brownhills. The No. 8 was a Dennis Lance 1 double-decker, with Brush-built bodywork. It glided along with its quiet six-cylinder petrol engine hardly emitting any noise, in stark contrast to today's modern diesel buses. We approached Shelfield and just before the Spring Cottage public house, we paused to look down to the Leighswood branch railway line that passed through Shelfield from Leighswood sidings on the South Staffordshire line at Heath End, Pelsall, serving the various brickworks and collieries around Stubbers Green, Aldridge. As we watched, one of Ryecroft shed's Webb 0-6-0 coal engines, No. 28088, trundled by with a load of new house tiles. We were then greeted by an ex-North Walsall pupil named Alf, yelling as he passed by, driving his Dennis Lance 11, four-cylinder, double-decker bus No. 117, on his way back to Walsall on the 'Walsall Wood Dodger'.

We then approached Walsall Wood, passing over the narrow humpbacked bridge. We sighted a horse-drawn coal boat en route for the Birmingham area going along its way from Hednesford canal basin. It was an 'open Joey' boat named *Mary* with its open brazier freely smoking. Once over the canal bridge we passed along the High Street with its many trim, clean-looking shops to reach the old Walsall Wood station. By then Walsall Wood was closed to passenger trains, but we were able to see one of the many mineral trains that passed by from the Cannock Chase sidings via Norton Pool, (now known as Chasewater), to Aldridge. The ex-Midland class 3 locomotive, No. 3502 of Ryecroft shed, was on this particular train. The No. 16 bus from Lichfield to Walsall then drifted down from Shire Oak Hill; it was AEC Regent petrol bus No. 59. We then had to climb for almost one mile to the summit of Shire Oak. We paused at the traffic lights while two of Pickfords' chain-driven heavy lorries crawled up the steep hill from Brownhills, carrying a heavy load of machinery.

The cycle ride to Lichfield, from the summit of Shire Oak with its pleasant countryside, made a very welcome change to lads so used to living in industrial areas. From this point on the three spires of Lichfield Cathedral could be seen, now only some six miles distant. Descending the long, steep slope of Shire Oak Hill, the air always seemed to smell fresher somehow, in strong contrast to the Black Country side of the hill. We arrived at the Boat Inn, stopped and went down to the canal that ran from Ogley Hay down to Huddlesford. Some of the North Walsall boys who came with us stopped here to enjoy another hobby, a day's fishing. We said 'Cheerio' and cycled away to Muckley Corner. This was, even then, a fairly busy crossroads, with Walsall to Lichfield traffic being required to halt at the 'Major Road Ahead' sign. It was no problem to cross the A5 in those days. We had to wait for a few seconds for a five-ton Morris commercial lorry and a small Austin 7 'Chummy' car to pass, these being the only vehicles then in sight on the A5.

About two minutes' cycling then brought us to the South Staffordshire Water Company's pumping station on the approaches to Pipe Hill. We stopped to admire this pumping house of Victorian vintage with its walls covered in ivy. Through the large glass windows we could see a huge flywheel turning slowly. Curiosity getting the better of us this particular day, we rode down the gravel path leading up to the pumping house. The attendant advanced purposefully towards us, intent on seeing us off his territory very smartly. Explaining our wish merely to see inside the pumping station, we were allowed just to peep inside for a few brief moments. It was a marvellous sight to behold, the steam engine driving the flywheel, some fifteen feet in diameter, slowly round. Only a slight hissing sound came from the piston. This, accompanied by a slight cuff and swishing

Walsall Wood, early twentieth century. Walsall Wood was once part of Cannock forest. Walsall Wood Colliery opened in the late 1870s. The population grew from 1891 to 1921 mainly due to coal mining and brick making. The village developed particularly from the end of the century. A station opened in High Street when a passenger service was introduced in 1884. This was withdrawn in 1930.

Shire Oak public house, c. 1920. A tree called the Shire Oak stood where the north-east boundary of Walsall Wood crosses the Walsall to Lichfield Road. Mention of the tree occurs in 1533 and the remains of it were removed in the mid-1890s.

Aerial view of Walsall, 1926. This shows the London Saddlery Company in Goodall Street and the Lichfield Brewery Company in Freer Street. Goodall Street, with Freer Street running off it, was built between High Street and Bridge Street in the 1830s.

Bridge Street, 1927. This shows the corner of Bridge Street before widening. Bridge Street was constructed in 1766 to connect the centre of the town with Ablewell Street. During the inter-war years (1918-1939) vast reconstruction schemes were undertaken in Walsall. One of the chief features of these was the widening of Bridge Street, which was completed in 1932.

sound, was all that was to be heard. The interior of the building was immaculate, with brasswork gleaming in the gloomy interior. The shafts of sunlight through the windows piercing the gloom reflected eerily on the movement of the rotating flywheel. We looked through a rear window to see a man unloading a coal barge to help feed the boilers that kept this monster working. We left after thanking the attendant and rode towards Pipe Hill. Here we crossed the railway and canal bridge, in time to see one of Bescot's G1 locomotives, No. 9328, making heavy going up the gradient from Lichfield city to Brownhills, with a heavy load of freight from Wychnor Junction.

We sped down Pipe Hill into Lichfield, calling in at a very small sweet shop in Bore Street for a glass of pop. Nearby was Lichfield Cathedral. But not for us was the architectural grandeur of this masterpiece or any of Lichfield's other historical buildings. A North Walsall schoolmistress, a Miss White, once asked in class if any of us knew Lichfield and its historical attractions and was quite taken aback to find that most of her boys regarded Lichfield Trent Valley station as the most important building in Lichfield. We cycled up Tamworth Street hill to join a traffic jam, caused by loose cattle going to the Smithfield cattle market in Church Street. In the hold up was a Midland Red Q-type S-0-S single-deck petrol bus. With its bright red paintwork and aluminium-painted roof glistening in the bright sunlight, and its petrol engine puffing smoothly, it was a tribute to the high standard of maintenance prevailing in those pre-war days. We managed to pass the traffic jam and cycle out of Church Street into the old Burton Road to eventually reach our goal, Lichfield Trent Valley station. This was a source of entertainment for many schoolboys. This place ranked far superior to any theatre, cinema, fair or day trips with parents. A pathway led from the old Burton Road bridge to platform 1 on the down side of Lichfield Trent Valley station. Alongside was a grass bank some six feet high, very nicely situated for viewing the main line and high-level station. It was not uncommon on a hot summer's day to see some hundred or more schoolboys sitting peacefully on the bank with pencils and paper, bottles of pop and sandwiches. Grass along the top of the bank was very sparse indeed, with the concentrated movement of backsides over the years. None of the lads engaged in any form of vandalism or mischief. They were just content to watch the passing trains. Many friendships were made with schoolboys from Burton-on-Trent, Birmingham and other districts, who made the regular pilgrimage to this trainspotter's mecca. With expresses passing every few minutes under the three bridges of the station confines, we were amazed by the birds that chose to nest under the bridge arches, with the exhaust of locomotives blasting underneath every few minutes twenty-four hours a day.

The year 1937 saw the introduction of the new LMS streamlined *Coronation Scot* running between London and Glasgow. The down one passed Lichfield at approximately 2.00 p.m. and the up train at 6.00 p.m. During that Coronation-year summer, many adults, with families, went to Trent Valley station, resulting in some hundreds of people lining both platforms and the surrounding viewpoints. The sight of locomotives Nos 6220 *Coronation*, 6221 *Queen Elizabeth*, 6222 *Queen Mary* and 6233 *Princess Alexandra*, of the first batch made at Crewe, painted in blue and white, brought cheering and waving from this large gathering of people and schoolchildren. The never-ending procession of expresses continued steaming by at approximately 70mph, including the Royal Scot, Midday Scot and the Irish Mail. Into our notebooks were jotted Royal Scots, Princess Royals, Jubilees, Patriots and Black Fives.

The old South Staffordshire line, running across the main line, was not so interesting. It was very rare to see a named locomotive on this line, but, nevertheless, the numbers

Blue Coat School, pre-1934. The school was demolished in 1933 to be replaced by the central station. It had been built in 1859. It was in the early English style with carving which included the bear and ragged staff, a blacksmith and anvil and one king and two queens. The tower was surmounted by a massive stone cap and an octagonal spire.

Green Lane, looking north towards Blue Lane crossing, 1938. Birchills Lane, which was also known as Green Lane, is mentioned in the sixteenth century. It was developing as an industrial area by the second half of the eighteenth century with many metal workers living there. The canal came here at the end of the century. The area has remained industrialised.

of G1s, tank engines and Midland class 2, 3 and 4 engines helped to make up our lists. We made a few trips to the down platform tap to fill our pop bottles with water. This was to coincide with the arrival of a Rugby-Crewe local. At this time the locomotive was usually a Prince of Wales class from the Stafford shed, but occasionally one of the new Stanier tank engines would put in an appearance. On this particular day it was hauled by No. 25674 *Scott*; the local was booked to stop for some time to allow the passage of a main line express along with a top line connection with a Walsall to Burton local. The activity on the platform was tremendous, some thirty or more passengers joined the train and a similar number alighted. The guard and porters then proceeded to move parcels and milk churns that had been deposited the platform length. On the engine the fireman was busy raking coal down the tender with the driver leaning out of his cab. We engaged in conversation with the driver and asked him why he had not got one of the new Stanier tank engines today. He retorted that Stafford shed was the dumping ground for old time-expired LNWR engines sent down from Crewe, but that occasionally they borrowed one of the new tanks or Black Fives and held on to them if possible. As he spoke an up express thundered by and our Stafford friend said cheerio, as he was given the road with his local in the wake of the express. He opened the regulator of *Scott* and blasted his way towards his next stop at Armitage. On the high-level down line an empty cattle train arrived to take water hauled by a Stanier Black Five No. 5033. It had just collected a train of fresh, clean cattle vans from the Lichfield city cleaning department. The system was for all fouled cattle vans from the Midland goods yards to be shunted to Lichfield for cleaning prior to their return to the main line and back to Holyhead for a fresh consignment of cattle. No. 5033 had arrived tender-first from Lichfield city. After taking water it ran round its train and, after passing Trent Valley top-line signal box, it descended the curve down to the low-level starting signal for the down main line. As it awaited the road, it stood with the fine Trent Valley Maltings buildings in the background, with its very pleasant aroma.

A very sprightly and tidy gentleman of some seventy years engaged us in conversation. He turned out to be a retired signalman with some forty-five years service on the Trent Valley signal boxes from Stafford to Tamworth. He was a mine of information and proceeded to explain the various bell codes that rang incessantly from Trent Valley signal box. He recalled the many hours spent in this box and other boxes along the Trent Valley line, working as a relief signalman. The Trent Valley box was, in the 1930s, double manned, such was the volume of traffic. Its position between the up and down fast lines was precarious, with only a few inches distance between passing expresses thundering by at 70mph. Looking from the box towards the north there was a splendid view of the Trent Valley Maltings situated on the Lichfield-Burton Road. From this malthouse the pleasant aroma of yeast drifted on the fresh Trent Valley air. After an interlude with our retired signalman, from whom we extended our knowledge of railway administration, we embarked on a diversion for refreshments. That involved a quick spin on our bikes to the public house situated in the hamlet of Huddlesford, approximately one mile away. We used to go round to the back door of the pub to buy pop, which we enjoyed sitting in a pleasant garden overlooking the canal from Fradley to Coventry. At this point the main line crossed the canal, so no engine names or numbers were missed. A sight I remember to this day was a horse drawing a coal-boat, gently plodding on its way from Nottingham coalfields to the Coventry industrial area. At about the same time as this boat passed at its leisurely 4mph, a Royal Scot class engine No. 6142, *The York and Lancaster Regiment*, passed above it at approximately 75mph, hauling a fourteen-coach up Blackpool to London express.

Walsall gas works in the first stage of demolition, c. 1978. The first gas works opened in Walsall in 1826. A new works opened in 1850 and in 1877 the main operation moved from Wolverhampton Street to a site at Pleck, shown here.

After our refreshments, we cycled back to Lichfield Trent Valley station. Towards teatime, traffic along this main line increased. Between Armitage and Tamworth there was only one up and down line. This was a bottleneck that must have stretched the wits of the signalmen on this ten-mile stretch. They had to keep proper margins especially with regard to fitting freight trains in between the expresses. One train we saw was a cattle train with some forty vans that used to wait on the up slow lines at Armitage for an up express, then it would be switched into its wake to make the up slow line at Tamworth. It was quite a sight to see it passing Lichfield, usually hauled by a Black Five Stanier at about 60mph, its swaying and lurching vans of cattle mooing and bumping together as they headed south from Holyhead after a boat trip from Ireland, to finish up in London butcher's shops. These poor creatures must have suffered before going to their fate.

We also saw several freight trains hauled by the ex-LNWR G2A Super D class locomotives scurrying after expresses on both up and down lines on the Armitage-Tamworth bottleneck. They were often hauling in the region of 500 tons as they came lurching and rocking at speeds of up to 60mph, with clattering coupling rods flying round their little four-feet five-inch driving wheels. By teatime traffic had become very busy on the main line and also on the high level. Local passenger trains on the Lichfield Trent Valley to Birmingham via Sutton Coldfield and Walsall line ran around the trains for the evening rush hour. Each local train, including those running direct from Derby to Birmingham and Walsall, disgorged vast amounts of parcel traffic, to be transhipped from high level to low level and vice versa. We lads watched this operation, as trolleys loaded to the maximum ascended and descended the water hydraulic lifts serving both up and down main and top lines. After hearing gurgling noises from the lift we enquired of the porter as to where the water pressure came from to work this crude but efficient lift. It ran by gravity from the canal by Pipe Hill pumping station.

As evening drew on and our notebooks began to fill with engine names and numbers, we began to say goodbye to our friends from various other schools within a fifty-mile radius of Lichfield Trent Valley station. We eventually decided to return to Walsall. One thing we often overlooked on our return trip was that it was a hard pull back with gradients against us until Shire Oak crossroads. An added factor was that we often had to contend with the western prevailing wind. One night we left late as we had been very reluctant to leave because each time an express on either up or down lines passed, the signal came off for another, such was the volume of traffic. We were always apprehensive of missing a named engine that we had not seen. Reluctantly we set off homewards and found to our consternation that the fresh wind was blowing against us. At the same time the light was starting to fade and our food and drink supply was nil.

Passing back through Lichfield on a late evening was usually a pleasant experience. The city somehow smelled different from Walsall. I suppose it was that Walsall was industrial, in contrast to Lichfield's upper-class environment and residential atmosphere. As we passed the Bowling Green Hotel, many customers were sitting drinking their pints outside in the cool evening setting sun. We still had sufficient energy to ascend Pipe Hill and as we descended the other side we saw the pumping station silhouetted against a very low sun on the horizon. Through the sunlit windows, flashes came from the perpetual motion of its huge flywheel. As we crossed the A5 road at Muckley Corner we waited for a solid-tyred Scammell lorry grinding along with a heavy load at about 10mph. Little did we realise that in forty-five years time these lorries would be hauling ninety per cent of the traffic that once went by rail. We moved on to the foot of Shire Oak Hill by a cottage, the owner of which catered for cyclists. After a whip-round amongst ourselves, we found the necessary coppers to purchase a bottle of pop and after each of us had had a swig we pedalled to the summit of Shire Oak, accompanied by burps and belches brought on by the pop's gases. We always made it a rule to climb Shire Oak as a matter of pride and achievement; no one got off to walk, for fear of ridicule. The sun had set as we freewheeled down to Walsall Wood and in the twilight the Black Country had a charm of its own, with factory chimneys smoking and foundry cupolas lighting the sky in preparation for the night shift.

Top of Ablewell Street, 1936. This is a view looking down towards the town. As well as residential properties, occupants of the street at this time included the National Cash Register Company Ltd, Motor-Cycle Mart, Methodist Central Hall, Walsall Conduits Ltd, Atlas Malleable and General Ironworks and the Reliance Paint and Wallpaper Company.

It was completely dark as we reached Rushall and, as our cycle lights were almost non-existent, we dismounted and walked by Rushall county police station. These county police always seemed more strict than our own town police. In any case, there was always a constable to be seen in Rushall Square. We saw on this return journey most of the corporation buses which we had passed on our outward ride, each now with the late driver. Most of these bus drivers knew us lads, for the majority of them lived within the North Walsall and Birchills bus depot area. Arriving home, our parents gave us supper and packed us off to bed, somewhat mystified about the pleasure of spending almost ten hours cycling about twenty-five miles to collect names and numbers of railway engines. Still we were happy and contented and so engrossed in our hobby that mischief and vandalism did not even occur to us.

Looking back, the names of the engines did help our education when we returned to school. We often sought information from our teachers regarding the many and varied names bestowed on the locomotives. Their names came from members of the royal family, British colonies, warships, sea battles and regiments of the British Army. In the engine shed at Ryecroft, near the school, the LMS Company, during 1936 and 1937, allocated two 5XP Jubilee class engines the names Nos 5603 *Ceylon* and 5604 *Solomon Islands*. We mentioned this during a geography lesson to Miss White, our teacher, who was surprised to discover that the lads at North Walsall relished being taught geography, with the stimulus of spotting engines.

Above: *Digbeth and High Street, 1958. The Beehive (on the right of Mary Orton) was a household goods shop. The name may have derived from the shape of the building. Other occupants of the area in 1958 were a portrait photographer, a decorators' merchants, Walsall Wool Stores, a butcher, a jeweller and a silversmith.*

Opposite: *Old grocery shop, Wolverhampton Street, c. 1959.*

This concludes a typical trainspotting expedition to Lichfield Trent Valley. These trips to Lichfield took place at regular intervals, so I have compiled this particular chapter from many such outings. The references to engines and buses are of any that would be seen, but not on any given day. Still to this day, I can remember things in my mind to which I have referred and I hope I have conveyed a picture to anyone reading this of the happiness of the children of North Walsall junior and senior schools, with no aggravation or vandalism at the forefront of their minds. I and many of my ilk still paid visits to Lichfield Trent Valley until the demise of steam traction in 1964. Today some of us still visit the place just for a nostalgia trip, but viewing the new high-speed electric trains with their lack of character, as compared with the 'living' steam engines, leaves something to be desired. Yes, I think that the North Walsall lads were lucky to be able to make their own enjoyment within peaceful means. It was nice to have the freedom of the roads to cycle, and what few motorists there were always gave way to cyclists. We also did not have commercial television to tell us what to do.

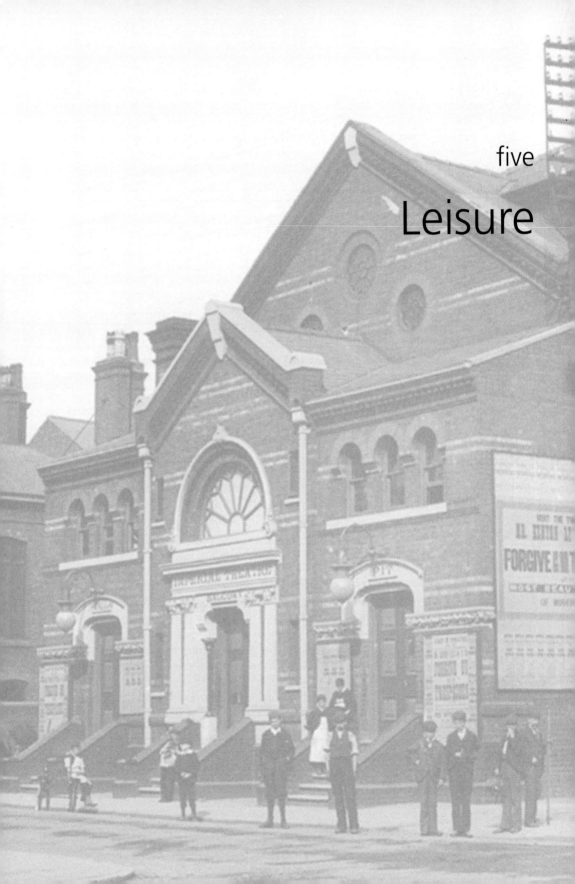

five

Leisure

My parents were regular customers at a very popular public house situated in Stafford Street called The Seven Stars. During the 1930s it had a most friendly proprietor, a Mrs Rose Bull. Life during the 1930s Depression was, to a point, grim. However regulars who managed to find surplus cash for a drink found solace in the company of Mrs Bull and her activities in promoting summer outings and Christmas parties for the women and children of her many working men regulars. I, as a small child of this era, was involved with the Bull family.

During the day most of the male customers were at work or seeking work. A few local foundries managed somehow to keep in business at this time, so during the lunch hour many workers called for a pint and a cheese sandwich to help replace sweat. These workers would occupy the main bar, which to my recollection was a male preserve. The rear bar was mainly used on Saturday or Sunday nights with wives accompanying their husbands. Just inside the main passage from the Stafford Street entrance between the two main bars was a small bar with about ten seats. This was used only for women and was referred to as The Snug. Us small children would be with our mothers in this Snug but were not allowed into the main bars. At the rear of the pub was the downstairs living accommodation for the Bull family – wife, husband and two daughters – with bedrooms above upstairs. A large yard was at the rear, that was useful to put us children out to play in whilst mothers had their drink and engaged in the gossip of the day. This rear yard also contained a brewhouse that at times was used by Mrs Bull to brew her own sample of beer. To the rear of the Seven Stars pub was a very dirty, noisy foundry, and if the wind was in the pub's direction there was a very smoky environment. However this foundry supplied the Seven Stars pub with thirsty customers.

For us children and mothers, Mrs Bull was a very efficient organiser of a popular pastime of the 1930s: charabanc outings for her regulars during the summer months. She insisted on regular small payments from the male customers during the winter months and banked the money each week until the spring. Mrs Bull had a very strong friendship with the Dawson family who ran one of Walsall's pioneer charabanc and motor coach businesses. Thus with money saved in the winter months, a number of local coach outings became a regular feature in the pub's life in the 1930s. It was as a small child that I well remember going to the following places on what they called 'gypsy parties', Worcester with a steamer trip on the River Severn, Holt Fleet, Bridgenorth and Matlock. Two short trips were to Brewood and the Lickey Hills. All these evening and day trips had a focal point of a certain public house where Mrs Bull and the respective licensees had formed a victualler's friendship. My own experience of these pub visits was of playing in pub back yards with constant visits from parents fortifying us with numerous bottles of pop and Vimto, plus endless packets of Smith's crisps. Pubs closed in those days at 2.00 p.m. Then we would explore the local town until teatime. The route was then to return to the pub again from 6.00 p.m. for approximately one hour then make for home. By this time the ladies would be in a state of merriment. Most of them would have purchased a 'kazoo', a small tin instrument that made a sound you could normally make blowing on a comb wrapped with tissue paper. So as Alec Dawson drove his charabanc homewards he would be distracted by certain merry females dancing in the gangway, lifting their skirts to the cacophony of blasting kazoos played out of tune. With luck, in the 1930s a coach driver could almost have the road to himself, only the occasional passing car or bus would be in evidence. When out in the country, Alec Dawson would be requested

Seven Stars public house, Stafford Street, twentieth century. In 1925 Rose Bull was the owner and licensee. There was a brewing plant, public bar, smoke room and three bedrooms. A survey of 1932 reported that the brewhouse was still in use. The public house was sold in 1980.

A charabanc outing outside Eyland & Sons' factory in Lower Rushall Street, c. 1920. Charabanc outings were very popular in the 1920s and 1930s when few people had cars. Trips did not go very far afield. Destinations included Brewood for an evening trip and Bridgenorth, Matlock and Worcester for longer trips. Eyland & Sons was established in 1790.

to make an emergency stop. The ladies, after consuming above the normal amount of ale, plus excitement, would all retire to a suitable field with hedgerows to attend to nature's demands accompanied by screams of laughter and rude remarks. In the back of the charabanc the ladies would commence dancing and singing the popular songs of the day, not always in harmony. By the time Walsall was reached, most of the ladies would be sitting exhausted in their seats, with most of us small children fast asleep. Sometime approaching midnight the coach would arrive back at the Seven Stars pub where dutiful husbands would be waiting for their wives and children, most of whom had to be carried home by dad.

Mrs Bull would finally see off all her party and would make sure that Alec Dawson's coach was left in good condition. He would be handed a tip for his safe driving and patience with these merry females, then head back to his navigation garage. Thus finished one of many pub 'gypsy parties' that were a regular event in the 1930s with the innovation of reliable motor coaches. Looking back it gave an opportunity for working-class women to escape the hard times and reality of those uncertain pre-Second World War years.

With the advent of the Second World War this way of life came to an abrupt end and my parents only visited the Seven Stars occasionally. I, myself, never again saw Mrs Bull, who was nearing retiring age. I was away from Walsall in the forces from 1945. Upon coming home on leave one evening on the 118 Birmingham Midland Red Bus I was reading the *Evening Dispatch* paper. To my horror I read that Mrs Bull, late licensee of the Seven Stars public house, had committed suicide in the canal in Birmingham Road that I had just passed. This was a sad end to a lady who was always the life and soul of the party.

The wireless

Life in the 1920s and early 1930s was, to say the least, a struggle for working-class people (that is to say, those lucky enough to be in a job). Only the rich could afford the luxury of a car or to take regular holidays. The working classes could occasionally scrounge a few shillings for a visit to a theatre or a silent film, and later, to see a talking picture.

In 1923 the British Broadcasting Corporation started transmission. My father was one of the first to own a crystal set, which was very primitive. It was an achievement to get decent reception by twisting the knobs to line up the cat's whisker, while at the same time holding on to the flimsy earphones. He decided to wait, for manufacturers had forecast great advances in radio reception in the next few years. Some battery operated sets came on the market, but the heavy accumulator had to be taken to a wireless shop for recharging every few weeks. My father decided to wait until new electrical sets became available. There was also a problem of being able to afford one during the Depression.

It was not until the early 1930s that the working man had the option to purchase a radio set. The government allowed businessmen to sell the new radios on very generous hire purchase terms. In the case of my father, who was in a regular job bringing home approximately £2 10s per week, rent, food, clothing and fuel amounted to just over £2, leaving very little for a weekly visit to the pub and a packet of Woodbine cigarettes a day. Most of our neighbours in Webster Road were living in similar circumstances, but from about 1934, when one of these neighbours acquired one of the new radios, costing in the region of £10, others strove to emulate him and by the outbreak of the Second World War almost every working-class home could boast an electric radio set.

My father decided to own a radio and this he achieved by saving money from working overtime. Being employed by Walsall Corporation Transport as a general handyman, sometimes he was lucky to get a few hours' overtime despite the rigid fixed working hours, under corporation restraint owing to the Depression. The best means of procuring overtime came when certain sections of the trolleybus wiring system from Bloxwich to Willenhall had to be renewed. This procedure took place after the last trolleybuses ran, about midnight on Saturday, until the first bus on Sunday morning. Sometimes, if problems arose, men would work until midday Sunday with petrol buses working the service. Double time was paid for this but not many men relished a night out in varied weather conditions, so a few regulars, including my father, became the usual volunteers.

Another cold, vile night job that brought in extra cash was during heavy snowfalls. This entailed the fitting of skid chains to the rear wheels of buses. This applied to buses working on the exposed Cannock Chase routes. After the bad winter of 1934, my father went to one of the dealers in the then new wireless trade. He decided to patronise a certain Mr Frank Mander who had just opened a wireless shop in West Bromwich Street, Caldmore. To say Frank Mander was fully skilled in the world of electronics is an understatement. After he had closed down his shop, when radios had lost their popularity to the television, and despite soon mastering the art of television repairs, Frank was offered a very lucrative job appertaining to wiring all electrical sections on the new M1 motorway from London to Birmingham. One Saturday afternoon in mid-1934, I went with father to purchase a new wireless set from Frank Mander. On his recommendation, we purchased a model of Cossor manufacture known as a Six-Valve, Three-Waveband Superhet Wireless. It was a very sophisticated work of engineering and Frank Mander informed us that it would last us a number of years. This was an understatement, for the set is still in use today. My father carried the new wireless home on the bus (only the large businesses could provide a horse and cart or a new motor van in those pre-war days). When we had found a place for it on the sideboard, it was indeed a fine piece of furniture by virtue of its hand-built mahogany cabinet, with a glistening layer of varnish. Mother was thrilled with the acquisition but queried about the cost. This Cossor radio was priced at nine guineas, with a down payment of ten shillings and then two shillings and sixpence per week to be handed over since my father could prove he was in regular employment.

Before our family could enjoy a listening session, two problems had to be overcome; a suitable aerial and earthing strip had to be fitted on the manufacturer's instructions. We had to purchase a wooden wireless pole, some ten feet high which was placed at the bottom of our garden, some thirty feet from the house. After digging a hole five foot deep, the heavy pole was manhandled into the hole with the kind assistance of our neighbours, then it was supported by heavy stones mixed with cement. When this was erected, the copper-wired aerial was stretched into the council house rafters, then via the front of the house, through a hole drilled into the window frame. News then spread around the neighbouring streets that, 'The Haddocks were on the air'. With everyone local acquiring wireless sets, it was very comical to see almost every house with their high wireless poles and aerials standing proud. The local bird population found the aerials most useful vantage points to look down on marauding cats, before swooping down for breadcrumbs that housewives threw out.

All these primitive wireless sets (by today's standards) required an earthing system at the manufacturer's insistence. To ensure a positive earth, my father dug a hole three feet deep to place a large copper cable consisting of worn-out trolleybus wire attached to the

Jack Haddock's wireless. This wireless was purchased in 1934 and is still working in 2004. It was described in 1934 as a model of Cossor manufacture known as a Six-Valve, Three-Waveband, Superhet Wireless. The chance to purchase such sets provided a new source of entertainment and information for many working people.

small earth wire from the mains set via another small hole next to the aerial hole in the window frame. When Webster Road council houses were modernized in 1980, the men who had to fit the new window frames were puzzled by the old window frames each having two holes situated in the bottom right-hand corner. When I explained to them about the early 1930s wireless age, I became suddenly aware of the progress since the 1930s. Now we are in the new era of television and videos.

Before we could start listening to our new radio, father had to buy a receiving licence from our local post office for the princely sum of £1. Thus we commenced to familiarise ourselves with the range of programmes available. The BBC was indeed very sombre and formal, ruled by the governor of the BBC, John Reith, later Sir John Reith, along with his fellow directors who were mainly prominent members of the clergy, including several bishops. We soon became aware of this situation by virtue of Sunday broadcasting. The day's programmes consisted of church service recordings, classical music with special emphasis on composers like Bach, and the choirs of famous cathedrals such as Canterbury and York. News programmes and talks on current affairs made up a solemn day's broadcasting, with the one highlight of the day being the visit to the Grand Hotel, Eastbourne, Sussex, for a concert given by the Palm Court Orchestra, led by Albert Sadler. The music was from musical comedies like *The Desert Song* or music of the Strauss family. One Sunday evening programme that I remember was *The week's Good Cause*, detailing gifts to charities and hospitals by prominent men from all walks of life. Sunday night closedown took place about 11.00 p.m. after the epilogue.

The mid-week broadcasts consisted of news, drama and current affairs programmes during the day but, with men at work and mothers attending to domestic matters and looking after children, it was the evening programmes that were most eagerly looked forward to. Variety shows became a regular feature, with well-known music hall artistes trying to adapt to the transition from stage to the studio with its microphones. Most of them seemed very subdued as rules forbade any smut or potentially offensive jokes. We used to listen to Max Miller until he passed a rather suggestive blue joke and was promptly banned from radio. Perhaps Saturday night was the most entertaining, with broadcasting until almost midnight. The dance bands of Jack Hylton, Jack Payne, Henry Hall, Roy Fox and Harry Roy were most popular. The national waveband was the main programme, but at times the regional waveband could be heard. We in the Midlands tuned in to Daventry. Two dance bands heard on the Midland Region that were very popular with listeners were Billy Merrin and his Commanders from a well-known Nottingham ballroom, and Hermann Darewski from Trentham Gardens ballroom near Stoke-on-Trent.

One innovation in broadcasting during the mid-1930s that had listeners glued to their radios was outside broadcasting. Most households with sets became spellbound listening to the Aldershot Military Tattoo. A most interesting outside broadcast was a midsummer visit just before midnight to a woodland location to hear the nightingale in full song. Both these programmes became the topic of the day amongst factory workers and school children the morning after. Our wireless was on the air continually from teatime to closedown, likewise our neighbours were in a similar situation and meeting them in the street the topic of programmes came under much speculation.

Our listening was not always confined to the BBC. Reception from the Continent was very good and at times one could hear America. We soon discovered, on the short wave band, amateurs who would be broadcasting between one another at regular times. It was most interesting to listen to the gossip, although it consisted mainly of technical jargon.

Above left: *Cutting from the* Walsall Observer, *5 January 1935. This was the heyday of the cinema, when a town like Walsall could support several cinemas in the town centre. The Electric Picture Palace in the Square opened in April 1910. It could seat 1,000 people. By 1922 it was just the Palace. It had a number of owners. The ABC took it over in 1936. It closed in 1955. (Reproduced by courtesy of the* Walsall Observer.)

Above right: *The Imperial Theatre, Darwall Street, early twentieth century. The Imperial started off as the Agricultural Hall. It was the first cinema in Walsall, showing films in 1908. Talkies came in 1930 with* All Quiet on the Western Front. *The Imperial became a bingo hall in 1968 and is now a public house.*

Once I heard an amateur from Canada broadcasting to someone in England and heard a Canadian Pacific train passing his house with noise from its exhaust and chime whistle blowing off. I believe this long-distance reception depended on favourable weather conditions.

It did not take us long to discover the well-known commercial station, Radio Luxembourg. It was most welcome to listen to innovations such as American jazz music with programmes sponsored by the likes of Ingersol watches, Ovaltine and other well-known food companies. The Ovaltine programme was for children's benefit and had its own signature tune, 'We are the Ovaltinees little boys and girls'. Most of us children wrote to Radio Luxembourg to join its club and they posted badges advertising their products. Children had a mania for sporting as many badges on their jackets as possible. This badge craze seemed to die out with the advent of the Second World War. One chewing gum programme supplied lads with a badge portraying a football with words describing the eleven team positions. In our school the centre forward badge accounted for most of the lads. The BBC, however, produced a very good formal programme for children called *Children's Hour*, broadcast between 5.00 and 6.00 p.m. each week day, edited by an Uncle Mac, with the emphasis on knowledge as opposed to Luxembourg's somewhat gimmicky output.

A programme which was most popular at the time was *Monday Night at Eight* by Harry S. Pepper, a well-known producer. Its contents consisted of popular music hall artistes, along with dance bands playing the latest hits. Most families listened to this programme, which finished at 9.00 p.m. In our street at this time most of the male population would

Science and Art Institute, Bradford Place, 1935. The institute opened in 1888. It was damaged in the Zeppelin raid on Walsall in 1916. An eye witness had to be stitched up by a doctor because of the wounds he received. The institute continued in use until the end of the twentieth century. In 1974 it was a centre for training in making leather goods.

then be seen trekking to the North Walsall Working Men's Club or local public houses. Saturday evening at 6.00 p.m. was responsible for a mass tune in for *In Town Tonight*, which portrayed life in our capital city. Its main content was interviews with famous people from all over the world who were visiting London, plus some interviews with working people such as London bus drivers or market people. It is still remembered today by people over fifty years of age for its signature tune *Knightsbridge*, by Eric Coates, a well-known English composer. Two sporting events that would empty the streets before the Second World War were the boat race, with its commentator John Snagg, who only retired from this position in 1982, and the FA Cup Final. Today, in this television age, it is hard to imagine almost every household full to capacity with friends (some who did not possess a radio), listening to Raymond Glendenning's commentary, with the aid of a page of the *Radio Times* incorporating a plan of Wembley Stadium marked out in numbered squares in an effort to help listeners follow the field of play.

By 1939 the wireless was fast becoming a way of life for people from all walks of life, which was indeed uplifting and pleasant. This idyllic situation was somewhat shattered with the advent of the Second World War. Although our radios gave us great pleasure, most citizens were under no illusions as to what the future was to hold by listening to the news programmes dealing with Germany's occupation of various parts of Europe. The Nazi monster was about to drastically alter our new-found way of life and alter the ethics of broadcasting. On 3 September 1939 at 11.00 a.m. it is fair to say that every radio in the United Kingdom was tuned in to hear Prime Minister Neville Chamberlain declare war on Germany. After this dramatic announcement of hostilities with Germany again after twenty-one years of precarious peace and depression, most of our Webster Road citizens gathered together outside to discuss this historic event and at the same time to gather their wits and console each other. Our future was bleak and uncertain, which led to our wireless sets being tuned in to every bulletin in the hope that there would be news of England, France and Germany coming to some terms or compromise. However, it was to be war for the next six years and our wireless sets were to become a force indeed for raising our spirits and for information.

Interior of Her Majesty's Theatre of Varieties, 1937. The theatre, built in the French Renaissance style, stood at the bottom of Park Street and was an impressive local landmark. The auditorium was decorated in blue and cream and gilded plaster in the Louis XVI style. The stage was one of the largest in England. The theatre opened in 1900 and was demolished in 1937.

With the advent of 1940, nothing had happened on the Continent during the period known as the Phoney War. The first three months of 1940 brought in the most severe winter within living memory. With temperatures well below zero and heavy snowfall, it was a solace for families to huddle around their fireplaces and listen to the wireless. Spring of 1940 arrived, with the Hun invading the Low Countries and France, leading to Dunkirk and the Battle of Britain. This was England's darkest hour and through the medium of our wireless sets the civilian population was fully aware of the crisis that prevailed at this time, unlike our elderly citizens who pointed out to us that, during the First World War, news of events in France took weeks to be known via the newspapers.

Through our newspapers we were under no illusions as to the gravity of the situation. After the fall of France and the announcement that if church bells could be heard from all churches it was the signal that we were being invaded by the Germans (all church bells were ordered to be kept silent after the outbreak of war, only to be rung if invasion occurred) a National Government was formed with Winston Churchill as Prime Minister. He soon adopted the BBC as a means of informing the general public about our situation. On most Sunday evenings he spoke to the nation at 9.00 p.m. Every household would be tuned in to hear his famous patriotic speeches that inspired forces and civilians with the will to survive. In factories and shops the conversation on Monday about the Prime Minister's speech lasted all day and most of the following week. We all became very thankful for our wireless sets. Another famous orator who uplifted the population was the well-known American journalist Quinton Reynolds, who specialised in slinging his sarcastic wit towards Adolf Hitler and his fellow henchmen. In the heat of the Battle of Britain a new method of broadcasting appeared in our homes. War correspondents became well known as they brought the war to us virtually as it happened. One fond memory of this new procedure, which I well remember, was listening to a live commentary by, I believe, Godfrey Talbot, describing a German air attack on shipping in the vicinity of Dover harbour which he recorded from a high vantage point on the white cliffs near to Dover's famous castle. This was the era of reports by Alan Moorhead, Wynford Vaughan Thomas and others. It was about this

Aerial view of Bridge Street and Lichfield Street, c. 1930. Lichfield Street was built from Bridge Street following an Act of 1830 and replaced Rushall Street and Dovegrove Street as the main road to Rushall and Lichfield. Building leases were granted from 1831 onwards. By the 1850s it was 'a street of remarkable beauty and not only the most picturesque but the most fashionable portion of the town'. (Reproduced by courtesy of Simmons Aerofilms.)

Upper Bridge Street, mid-twentieth century. The Bradford Arms shown here was on the corner of Bridge Street and Lower Rushall Street. Edward Burton was the owner in 1834. It closed in 1932 and the licence was transferred to the new Bradford Arms in Milton Street.

Lower Rushall Street, 1970. Eyland's factory was on the righ-hand side looking towards St Matthew's church. In 1962-63 the firm was making buckles, slides and ornaments for the belt, brace, surgical, millinery and shoe trades, together with cast wire and stamped articles for the leather, canvas and clothing trades. A residential development now occupies the factory site.

time that our Sunday broadcasts began to become more relaxed from the religious aspect. A famous variety show took to the air on Sunday nights called *Garrison Theatre* with Jack Warner, later to become a well-known film star. It was Forces entertainment that took priority from about 1940 onwards. The BBC at that time paid tribute every Sunday evening to all the European countries under Nazi occupation, by playing their respective national anthems, including those of Russia and the USA. On a summer evening while passing any street in town you could hear this patriotic tribute coming from open windows.

From 1940 until about mid-1944 we all suffered air raids, although Walsall's problems were minute compared with Birmingham and Coventry. Several citizens wired their air-raid shelters with an extension wireless speaker to the mains set. If my memory is right I believe that the BBC was not off the air during the London Blitz, but areas bombed had their power supplies cut off at times. Up to this time the wireless set was confined to the household until factories engaged on vital war work decided, with the BBC, to broadcast a programme called *Music While You Work* morning and afternoons, with famous dance bands taking turns to play to the workers. In no time at all factories large and small were equipped with extension speakers relayed from the office wireless. This procedure was a great success, for it led to increased production. I visited several factories during the war and wondered how some people acclimatised themselves to the noise of throbbing machinery in contrast to the dance band playing.

Most of the Webster Road residents tuned in at times to Radio Bremen and Hamburg to listen to the notorious traitor William Joyce, otherwise known as 'Lord Haw Haw'. His propaganda broadcasts aimed at demoralising the English were treated as a huge joke. While we were listening one evening with our neighbours, the Cooper family, Lord Haw Haw described Walsall in very great detail and mentioned Talbot Stead tube works in Green Lane. Some time later, in 1944, the Birchills district was the victim of an incendiary bomb raid. Some bombs did fall on Talbot Stead but they were quickly extinguished. However part of the nearby Birchills bus depot and Hawley's tent works in Bloxwich Road suffered severe fire damage.

Another German radio station we found amusing was one which had an announcer who did nothing but castigate British politicians with a flood of obscene language. His comments on Winston Churchill became a regular flood of filthy abuse. Our parents eventually found us listening to this nameless person and promptly banned us from doing so.

As the war progressed, listening to the BBC, we became aware of a gradual change from the old puritanical style of radio, as laid down by John Reith. Towards the end of the Second World War, variety shows could be heard on Sunday evenings with comedians passing nearly blue jokes that would previously have been banned. I think the peak of listeners tuning in to the BBC was on 6 June 1944, D-Day. Men on their way to work just after 6.00 a.m. heard the announcement of the invasion of France. For a change this gave the housewives something important to gossip about. As each bulletin was announced throughout the day, they rushed to meet in groups and engage in serious discussion, leaving any local scandal and domestic events alone for once. When my father and our neighbours came home from work, they took over from the women, just listening, glued to their sets, speculating about the situation. So it was that almost everyone's wireless was on from about 6.00 a.m. until midnight. I remember my father telling me to place my hands on the radio cabinet just before midnight and it was almost red hot, just like a radiator.

It was just as well that we working-class families purchased wireless sets prior to the war, for, with the emphasis on demand for wireless communications to aid the war effort, it

Stafford Street and Wisemore, 1936. By the 1830s this area to the east of Townend Bank was densely built up. It was cleared in the 1930s and much of it was obliterated for the building of Walsall Technical College, 1949-1969.

Stafford Street and Littleton Street junction, c. 1960. On the right is the Baptist chapel opened in 1847. It was enlarged in 1869 but replaced by a new building in Green Lane in 1972. Beyond is the area now occupied by a car park.

became almost impossible to purchase a new radio. The war progressed in our favour and as VE Day arrived some of our radios were then approaching ten years of age.

From about this time, until the advent of television in the early 1950s, local residents tuned in regularly to the comedy programmes that are still well-remembered today by anyone over fifty. Who can forget the famous Liverpool comedian Tommy Handley with his show *ITMA* (*It's That Man Again*). This programme was probably the best from the golden age of radio comedy that survived well into the new television era. My memory of this Cossor radio ends with listening to programmes such as the *Goon Show* (an unforgettable classic), *Much Binding in the Marsh* and *Take it from Here*. My father passed away in 1953 and, looking back, his wireless was money well spent. It was not much used after 1960, as television reigned supreme thereafter. The Cossor radio is still working today but has a faulty valve, which I hope to have replaced by a specialist radio firm. While examining this valve it occurred to me that today you can purchase a small transistor radio, that is smaller than one of these 1934 Cossor Superhet valves.

On the 50th anniversary of Mr Neville Chamberlain's speech declaring war on Germany on 3 September 1939, the programme was repeated. I listened to it on the original Cossor radio, which was still working in September 2002.

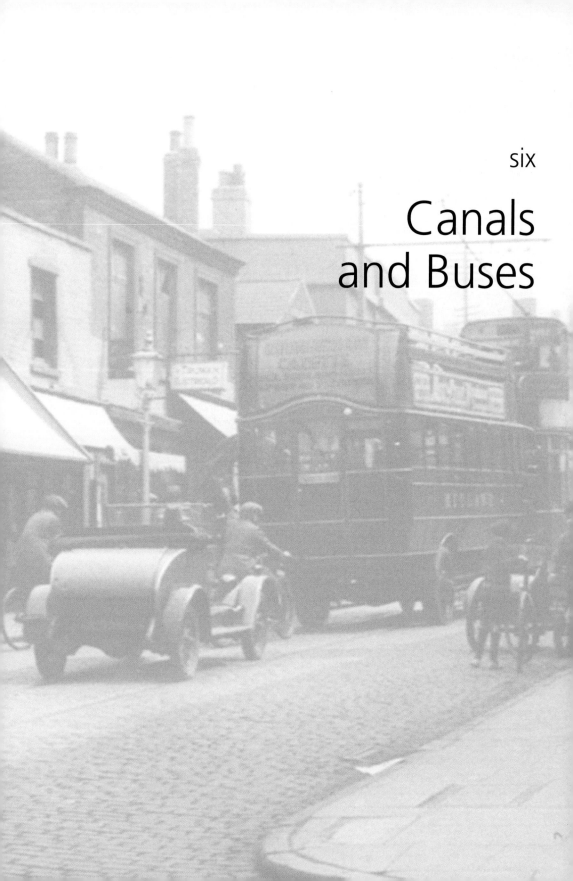

six

Canals
and Buses

The flying canal boatmen

Life was full of uncertainty during the Depression for the working man as there were long periods of unemployment. What jobs were available were poorly paid and one was subjected to the moods and whims of the employer. No Social Security system or health and safety regulations were available in the various industries or workplaces. This story relates to the canal transport firm of Ernest Thomas & Son, boat builders and canal haulage proprietors and his workforce. These men had a hard life, existing on low wages, with very little time for recreation. The public house was their main outlet for relaxation. Ernie Thomas was a hard taskmaster to his employees. He was not alone in this respect, almost all employers during the 1930s revelled in their authority. The working man was expected to do a fair day's work and could be dismissed for even a trivial misdemeanour. There was plenty of skilled labour available at local Labour Exchanges. When Ernie Thomas was asked about working conditions and pay structure, his reply would be: 'I am the piper and I play the tune'. Nevertheless, most of his skilled boat builders and boatmen remained faithful to the company. Many times, loyal boatmen with large families when genuinely sick were rewarded with food hampers until they were fully fit to work. Just to survive during the 1930s Depression, those lucky enough to be in work, like Ernie Thomas's boatmen, accepted a hard day's work, with very little time for recreation or pleasure. They were only able to afford a night at the then new mode of entertainment, the cinema, or as cash would allow, the public house.

However, one day in July 1936, Ernie Thomas paid a visit to Walsall Aerodrome situated on the Aldridge Road to witness the visit of famous aviator, Alan Cobham's Flying Circus. Not many people could afford the entrance fee of five shillings, but many thousands watched from nearby roads and fields. These pioneer aviators performed many daredevil stunts. Ernie Thomas was making his way amongst the many monoplanes and biplanes on view when he came across a De Havilland two-seat Moth with a board advertising flights over Walsall for five shillings. No one seemed interested to take up this offer and Ernie Thomas enquired of a nearby aviator why there were no customers. The aviator was none other than Alan Cobham himself and he explained that not many people could afford the flight plus many were not willing to take a risk in the primitive biplanes of that era. Ernie Thomas was never backward in forming relationships with prominent people and soon acquainted himself with Alan Cobham's business routine. Ernie decided to assist Alan with his problem of encouraging potential flying passengers. He made his way to the local flying club's office in Bosty Lane and contacted his secretary, Miss Prescott, at Birchills canal boat dock. Ernie told Miss Prescott to instruct the firm's driver to load the Chevrolet lorry with as many boatmen as were available and drive them to Walsall Aerodrome. On arrival the men were informed that they were to sample a flight over the Walsall canal system, paid for by their employer. It was most fortunate that all working men wore flat caps in those days, as two were airsick and used their caps as receptacles and one was reported as having chewed part of his cap's lining. The pilot had evidently been instructed to loop the loop during each trip.

Back at the boat dock that day there were a lot of disorientated men amongst the workforce. However, the following day Alan Cobham rang Ernie Thomas with his thanks. Belief in the safety of passenger flight had been assisted as word of Ernie's 'flying boatmen' had spread around the town and many more customers arrived as confidence in flying became popularised. Ernie Thomas and Alan Cobham remained friends for many years and Ernie was thrilled when, after the Second World War, Alan was knighted for his services to aviation.

Horse-drawn fire engine, Birchills, 1928. The engine is being used at Ernie Thomas's boat dock, Birchills, to pump the coal wharfs to clean out surplus coal. It was loaned out by the fire brigade in its final days for such pumping tasks on the canal.

Ernie Thomas's boat dock, mid-1960s. In 1956 the firm was based at Old Birchills Wharf. Ernie Thomas started off as a coal merchant. The business developed after the Second World War when Ernie gained a large number of contracts to transport coal for power stations but declined in the 1980s when the power stations started to close.

Dennis single-deck Lancet petrol bus, 1939. This type of bus was used by Walsall Corporation in 1937 to convey Spanish refugee children from Southampton docks to Aldridge where they were housed at Aldridge Lodge. On the return journey a stop was made at Oxford where the local Co-op Society provided meals for the children and the staff with them.

Walsall Corporation Transport hire of buses for emergency and pleasure services

During the Spanish Civil War in 1937 the government authorised the evacuation of Basque refugee children to escape this most un-humanitarian conflict. Many towns were directed to accommodate and look after the needs and welfare of these unfortunate children and a number were sent to live at Aldridge Lodge in 1937. On 2 July 1937 Walsall Corporation Transport supplied a Dennis single-deck bus with two drivers, Mr Arthur Morrel and Mr William Hall, who had to report to Southampton docks where a special transit camp was in operation to distribute the various children. On arrival at Southampton, digs were provided for the drivers and arrangements were made for the bus to be serviced at Southampton Corporation municipal bus depot. Also, arrangements were made for a nurse to accompany the children on the return journey to Aldridge. A stop was made at Oxford where the local Co-op Society provided meals for the children and the bus drivers and nurse. On this particular day, Wolverhampton Corporation also provided a similar bus service for children allocated to Wolverhampton.

Walsall's town transport: The original St Paul's bus station

Walsall Corporation operated its first bus service on 23 May 1915 from Walsall to Hednesford via Cannock. From 1 January 1904 Walsall Corporation had taken over the running of all tramway routes in the borough from the South Staffordshire Tramways (lessee) Co. Ltd that operated within the Black Country conurbation. After the First World War all municipal transport undertakings began to realise the flexibility of buses in contrast to the limitations of trams, notwithstanding the financial and economic advantages. On 1 April 1933 the last tramway replacement took place and on 30 September 1933 Walsall Corporation ceased to operate tramcars, and trolleybuses replaced tramcars on the Bloxwich route and the joint Walsall to Wolverhampton service.

By 1934 Walsall Corporation had in service ninety-seven motorbuses and nineteen trolleybuses. Bus terminal points in 1934 were at Townend Bank for Wolverhampton

Bus at Fullbrook, c. 1937. Dennis 'E' type bus showing H 'Shiner' Shaw (driver) on the right. Fullbrook appears to have existed in the Middle Ages. Housing developed in the area in the 1930s. The corporation's use of motor buses expanded in the 1920s and 1930s. They were used to connect the new housing estates and other residential areas such as Fullbrook to the town centre.

(trolleybuses), Cannock, Hednesford and Pleck via Pleck Road and at Bradford Place for Wednesbury, Darlaston via Pleck, West Bromwich, Caldmore, Palfrey circular and Walstead Road routes. The Bloxwich and Leamore trolleybus routes terminated on Walsall Bridge, running via Townend Bank and Park Street. Bus terminals for Brownhills, Sutton Coldfield, Lichfield, Birmingham Road, Paddock Circular, Bloxwich and Blakenall, Cannock, Chasetown, Chase Terrace, Burntwood and Hednesford via Pelsall, Norton Canes and Heath Hayes were situated in either Darwall Street or Leicester Street.

With Birchills bus depot approximately one and a half miles distance from Walsall town centre, the Transport Manager became aware of dead non-profit mileage with buses operating morning and evening rush-hour services. In 1933 surplus land in Darwall Street between the post office and Walsall fire station was rented to park twelve buses.

The drivers and conductors travelled on the Bloxwich route to book off duty and deposit cash takings. This was a well-planned exercise by the management, stressing the need for economy during the 1930s Depression. Despite the uncertain financial situation at this time, the government of the day found finance to help relieve unemployment by patronising new council housing estates within the borough which led to expansion of new and extended bus routes. That required more buses, so the council and Transport Committee agreed to build a central bus station.

Most fortunately the old Blue Coat School in St Paul's Street was closing to move to a modern school in Springhill Road. The old school site was chosen for the new St Paul's bus station. On 5 February 1935 the Transport and Town Planning Committees met to consider plans for the layout of the bus station. Also, the Walsall Corporation Transport offices situated between the Imperial Cinema in Darwall Street and the Midland Bank on The Bridge were to be closed, with the new offices incorporated within the new bus station. The bus station lengths were to run from north to south and a garage was proposed to be erected over the bus station. Walsall-bound trolleybuses were to be diverted via Wisemore from Stafford Street to Walsall Bridge and were to depart via Park Street. These two options never materialised.

The new Bridge transport offices built adjacent to the Priory Hotel were indeed most luxurious, with a canopy on the frontage, modern toilets, inspector's department and a parcel office at ground level. Situated above were the general manager and assistant manager's offices. Most important were the wages and financial departments responsible

Hill Street, 1936. This was one of the two streets which led up from Ablewell Street to St Matthew's church. It housed several public houses, most of which were demolished in the 1930s. They included the Leathern Bottle, the Barley Mow and the original Queen's Head.

Upper Bridge Street, 1927. Walsall Co-operative Society had a base here which was expanded in the early 1930s. Other occupants of the street in the 1920s were the Singer Sewing Machine Company, the Walsall Fuel Supply Company, the Walsall Horse Collar Company and the fire station, Valuation Office, Surveyor of Taxes and the Inland Revenue Office.

The Bridge looking towards Park Street, c. 1930. Park Street once led to the ancient park in existence during the 1200s. In 1255 the park was owned by Geoffrey de Bakepus and was said to be full of deer and timber. The park was broken up prior to 1617 when a record from that time mentions the 'old gates of Walsall Park'. The Bridge and Park Street became the focal part of Walsall town centre from the nineteenth century onwards.

for all transport employees, including the Birchills depot staff. Birchills depot continued to deal with all conductors' ticket supplies for the appropriate routes and paying in after daily schedules. Prior to the official opening of the bus station, buses started to use the loading bays before the new transport offices were occupied. Transfer from the old offices took place on 19 July 1935. The new offices cost £16,378, plus £365 for the front canopy.

All buses arrived into the new bus station via Hatherton Road which was dual carriageway, with sufficient room for surplus buses to be parked along its length to St Paul's Street. The corporation terminated the rent of land in Darwall Street for bus parking. In any case the land was required for the construction of the new Darwall garage. Buses departed onto Walsall Bridge then via Lower Bridge Street for their destinations.

In 1950 some properties in Lower Stafford Street by the junction into Wisemore were demolished to enable the Bloxwich and Leamore trolleybuses to divert via St Paul's Street and terminate via a circle opposite St Paul's church and then use a surplus loading bay facing in a northerly direction. Over the years the original St Paul's bus station was tinkered with and modified slightly. This included replacing the original bus shelters, various refurbishments and repainting when CENTRO came into being. It had not been significantly altered until the last years of the twentieth century, when plans for a completely new bus station on the site came into being.

The controversial and futuristic new design has had its problems and building has undergone considerable delays, but it is now in operation, despite problems with the smaller 'satellite' bus station. Today, with this radical new 2000 bus station on the same site, the 1935 original is gone – but not forgotten!

Walsall Corporation Transport, 1930s: staff discipline

Walsall Corporation bus driver Jack Kelly was driving a single-deck Dennis Lance bus on the corporation's route No. 1 Walsall to Cannock and Hednesford. Single-deck buses were confined to this very well-patronised route because of the height restrictions, limiting high vehicles from passing under a railway bridge on the A34 at Churchbridge. Mr M.J. Somerfield, the general manager, lived along this route in Stafford Road, Bloxwich, and happened to be in his garden as Jack passed by driving the bus. Jack waved his hand in greeting to Mr Somerfield as he passed. The following day, Jack was summoned to Mr Somerfield's office and was severely reprimanded for removing his hand from the steering wheel whilst driving, thus endangering the lives of the passengers in his care. Jack could count himself lucky that he was only reprimanded, as Mr Somerfield was known to dismiss staff for the smallest misdemeanours. Mr Somerfield had served as a captain during the First World War and he used the same discipline with his employees at Walsall Corporation as he had used in the army. When Jack retired in 1969, he had amassed thirty-seven years' safe driving awards.

Harry Mason was a bus conductor in the 1930s and one day, while operating on route No. 23, Walsall to Brownhills' Rising Sun, he decided to make up his waybill on the return journey into Walsall. This would save him time when paying in on arrival at Birchills depot cash office. Not having many passengers on the bus that journey, Harry sat himself down in the vacant rear seat and calculated his cash accounts. The following day Harry was summoned to Mr Somerfield's office where he was confronted by the general manager with the fact that he had broken the company's rules by sitting down on duty.

High Street, 1936. On market days this area looking down towards Digbeth would have been full of stalls. Walsall's first surviving charter of c. 1225 granted permission for a market. The market days in the 1930s were Tuesday and Saturday. Premises on High Street in 1936 included The Harness and Saddlery Furnishing Trades Society & Metal Workers Association, Marsh & Baxter Ltd and Walsall Knitting Enterprise.

Harry was given a week's suspension from duty with loss of pay. It was many months later before Harry was to discover how the general manager knew of his misdemeanour. A fellow off-duty driver was cycling along the No. 23 route when he witnessed a bus inspector climbing the railway bank at Navigation Bridge on the Lichfield Road at Rushall. The inspector was obviously taking advantage of the tree cover along the bank so that he could actually spy on the buses as they passed by. It became apparent that this was a standard procedure ordered by Mr Somerfield himself. This practice of clandestine observations of traffic employees was authorised to occur at secluded points within Walsall Corporation's municipal bus network.

Of all Walsall Corporation's bus routes during the 1930s, the most despised route was the No. 26, Walsall to Birmingham Road Bell Inn terminus. The same dissatisfaction also applied to tramcar operation on this route. Although the route was only three miles in length, the problem was actually the passengers themselves. The most conservative and affluent of Walsall's residents lived along this route. Tram and bus conductors were subjected to many demands from these people. They regularly made complaints to the general manager. Sometimes the conductors would refer to the ladies as 'Luv' or 'Duck', which was quite acceptable on the friendlier working-class routes, where patter and banter between passengers was a commonplace occurrence. However, many conductors received suspension minus pay for this trivial misdemeanour. A bus driver or conductor with one button undone on their uniform or a driver applying the brakes a little too quickly would also be admonished. During the summer months working-class families from other areas of the borough would use the No. 26 route to visit the Bell Inn or the Australian Arms public houses. On the return journey, fortified with high spirits, this route would take on a different ambience, to which the elite locals did not take kindly. The police were often called because of passengers' behaviour. All Walsall Corporation personnel operated each route in turn but none was dreaded more than a week on the No. 26 route.

Digbeth, 1938. Digbeth was originally a raised path over marshy ground leading to the ford over the river. This view shows the entrance to the arcade on the right. Buxton & Bonnett have been in Digbeth since at least 1904. The radio shop may have been a response to the growing number of radio owners in the 1930s.

St Paul's Close, c. 1958. This street next to St Paul's church and parallel with Darwall Street has been all but obliterated by the new civic centre and other developments. It housed the office of the Earl of Bradford's agent in Walsall as well as insurance companies.

Dudley Street, 1930s. The Duke of York and White Swan public houses are shown decorated with bunting. The Duke of York was an old daub and wattle Tudor house. In 1925 it was in fairly good repair. It had a very small bar and smoke room but no lavatory or bathroom. It closed in 1937.

Lower Rushall Street, 1936. This is a view looking north from Ablewell Street. The buildings on the right-hand side have been replaced by a car park. Premises here in 1936 included a pawnbroker, a locksmith, a malleable iron founder and a currier.

Paddock Lane, 1936. Paddock and Wisemore were both names of common fields in Walsall in the Middle Ages. Paddock Lane existed by 1782. Development of workshops, factories and houses began in the 1850s. The building of multi-storey council flats in the 1960s split Paddock Lane and Tantarra Street in two. Metal and leather working were the main industries in the area in 1974.

seven

Walsall
Station

A short history of Walsall railway station

On 4 May 1837 the first railway line to pass near Walsall was opened. This was the Grand Junction Railway, running between Birmingham and Warrington. Now, in 1979, it is still the link from Bescot station to Darlaston, running alongside the M6 motorway and adjoining Pleck Park. All local railwaymen still refer to this line as 'The Old Road' or 'The Up and Down Grand'.

For a long time the nearest station to Walsall was at a point near the Walsall to Wednesbury Road. This station was called Bescot Bridge in the timetable, but it was also referred to as 'Walsall'. For passengers travelling to Walsall proper a coach service was provided, terminating at the George Hotel. This system was to last until 1 November 1847, when the South Staffordshire Railway opened a station in Bridgeman Place to link with the Grand Junction line at the present-day Bescot Junction. This first Walsall station was situated on the Pleck side of Bridgeman Street and was only a temporary structure, for by this time the South Staffordshire Railway was in the process of developing a line from Wichnor Junction to Dudley.

After 1847 Bescot Bridge station continued to be known by this name. During 1850 the LNWR, who had taken over the affairs of the Grand Junction Railway, closed the station. It was reopened on 1 February 1881 under the name of Wood Green. On 9 April 1849 the line from Wichnor Junction was opened and connected with the Bescot to Walsall section. On this day the first Walsall station was closed and the new one, in Station Street, was opened. This imposing building was not demolished until February 1978.

At first Walsall station had only one set of 'up and down' lines running through, but on 1 February 1861 the LNWR took over the South Staffordshire Railway and widened the station to allow passing lines to run through the centre. These were for mineral and freight trains, leaving two loops for passenger trains. This was typical LNWR practice to be found throughout their system. (Note: up lines are those running towards London, thus the Bridgeman Street end of Walsall station is the up side and the Park Street end is the down end.)

Walsall station concourse clock, 1977. This was part of the 1923 rebuilding. The main station entrance was in Park Street from 1883 after the station was rebuilt to cater for increased traffic. Passengers walked down a hallway from the concourse to the platforms.

Traffic soon began to increase for both passengers and goods. The opening of the Cannock line on 1 February 1858 and on to Rugeley on 7 November 1859 not only increased the number of passengers to Walsall, but also many small collieries began to move coal to Black Country regions. On 1 November 1872 the Wolverhampton line, via North Walsall, was opened by the Wolverhampton & Walsall Railway and the Midland Railway was by then negotiating for running rights to Walsall. By the time they finally established themselves in Walsall, in 1879, the station was already becoming seriously congested.

At about this time the station was being rebuilt and this work was completed on 1 November 1883. From this time the main entrance was from Park Street, with separate booking offices for the LNWR and Midland Railway companies. The station was owned by the LNWR and their stationmaster had complete control. The Midland Railway employed an agent who worked under the stationmaster's jurisdiction. The old South Staffordshire Railway building, in Station Street, was extended each side with LNWR-style brickwork. Passengers could still book or disembark from this old building, but most of its rooms were used for parcel traffic and administrative offices.

It was also at this time that the lines between platforms 1 and 2 were reduced from four to three. These formed the slow lines, with the middle line known as the 'down passing loop'. Between platforms 3 and 4 were the fast lines, with the 'town' side of platform 4 having the 'up fast loop' running beside it, giving another platform, number 5. There were also two short bays on the down side of the station. These bays, the 'Cannock' and 'Sutton' bays, were mostly used for parcel vans. The station was arranged in this fashion until the implementation of the Beeching Report on 18 January 1965.

At the turn of the century Walsall station was working to capacity. Approximately 1,000 train movements took place through the station in twenty-four hours. The railway gave much-needed employment to Walsall men, for the station payroll included guards, porters, shunters, clerks and officials, numbering well over 200.

One of the most important events in the history of Walsall station was the fire in Park Street booking hall on 25 March 1916. The roof was seriously affected, but no repairs could take place immediately owing to problems of labour and supplies during the First World War. With the aid of tarpaulins and general timber patchwork, a temporary repair had to suffice until hostilities ceased.

The iron and glass canopy over the Park Street entrance was not damaged by the fire and this structure was retained when work began on the new booking hall, after the war. The circular hall and concourse were erected by the LNWR local engineers. This imposing building was a brick structure, lined inside with oak. It was adorned with Grecian-style stone pillars and leaded windows in the roof. This booking hall was opened on 4 November 1923 by Mr J.F. Bradford, LNWR district superintendent.

From the late Victorian period until the Second World War, Walsall station was the hub of Walsall's trade, travel and commerce. The stationmaster was regarded as a very important person in the town, and he was always invited to public occasions. After the Second World War, with the growth of the motor industry, the station began to decline in importance. The quantity of passengers and freight began to fall off. This process was accelerated by the implementation of the Beeching Report in 1965, whereby all local passenger services, except the Walsall to Birmingham route, were axed.

This service was continually in danger of closing until 1977, when it was confirmed, although the half-hourly service was reduced to an hourly one. Apart from this, Walsall station was virtually dead. A short lease of life was granted with the rebuilding of

Interior view of South Staffordshire station building, 1978. This part of the building was used as the girls' dormitory for the restaurant staff. The restaurant opened in 1883. The restaurant staff was female, comprising a manageress, two cooks and on average a dozen waitresses and cleaners. The staff resided in this dormitory.

View from Walsall No. 2 signal box, Walsall station, 1975. Walsall station declined after 1965 and the implementation of the Beeching Report, which closed all local passenger services except that to Birmingham. This service was confirmed in 1977 and has since expanded from the one train an hour of that period.

Margaret Brotherton, ticket clerk, closing Walsall station concourse for the last time, 1978. The booking hall and concourse opened in 1923. They had had to be rebuilt after a fire in 1916. The building was a brick structure lined inside with oak. It had Grecian-style stone pillars and leaded roof windows.

Birmingham New Street station, around 1965–68, when Walsall had to handle all the diverted long-distance parcel trains. When New Street station was completed, Walsall's decline set in again until work began on the redevelopment of the site in February 1978.

The old South Staffordshire Railway buildings were demolished during February and March 1978 and, on 5 August 1978, the booking hall and concourse were closed, giving the staff one day to remove to temporary premises on platforms 2 and 3 and in Station Street. Demolition began on 9 August and was completed on 1 October 1978. The only part of the old station to be preserved was the canopy from the Park Street entrance, which was being stored by the borough parks department. The station redevelopment, begun in late 1978, included a £7 million shopping centre.

Carriage sidings

The first Walsall carriage sidings were situated in the area from Bradford Place to the station, backing on to the rear of Park Street. There were seven sidings which were constructed on the site of the old Walsall Racecourse Grandstand and were laid during the construction of the station in 1883. The first two sidings, adjacent to the up fast goods loop on platform 5, were exclusively for carriage storage and cleaning purposes. Sidings 3 to 6 were for use mainly for domestic coal supply to local traders plus other merchandise. Siding 7 was complete with a small covered fruit and potato shed. All these sidings were known as the 'back yard' to generations of railwaymen, and were known so until 1977, when the site was incorporated in the new Saddlers Centre shopping precinct. The only addition to the back yard sidings was when Sammons Brothers Ltd. rented, from the railway, a new, larger fruit and vegetable shed alongside the Bridgeman Street/Bradford Place side of the subway. Access to the back yard sidings onto the up and down fast lines was controlled by Walsall No. 2 signal box.

Midland yard shunt locomotive, Walsall station, 1956. The locomotive is taking water on platform 1, the down slow line. Up lines are those running towards London, thus the Bridgman Street end of Walsall station is the up side and the Park Street end is the down end.

A very large, high water tower was situated at the rear of the two carriage sidings, to the rear of the Park Street public house The Durham Ox. It had a water capacity of many thousands of gallons, which were pumped into the tank from the South Staffordshire Waterworks pipeline, constructed alongside the South Staffordshire Railway line from Wichnor to Dudley, when this line was opened in 1849. The function of the water tank was primarily to supply the hydraulic lifts on the station and three water columns for locomotive needs. The basement of the water tower housed the cleaning foreman's office, a large store and a mess room. A small brick building was attached to the mess room to accommodate a hot water boiler for cleaning the carriages. Before the advent of steam-heated railway carriages, this boiler house was used to store and fill a supply of tin foot warmers. During the winter period, a porter would have a regular job wheeling a trolley load of heated foot warmers to departing local passenger trains.

Considering that at the turn of the century Walsall station had just over 200 train departures and arrivals during a working day, the station welcomed the introduction of steam-heated stock during the early 1900s. The new bogie rolling stock was longer than the old LNWR six-wheel carriages. The new double four-wheel bogie stock was too long for the old back yard carriage sidings. Storing, wherever possible, these longer trains on spare goods roads temporarily solved the overcrowding problem. The situation was eventually solved when the old New Mills Midland Railway shed was finally closed in 1925, leaving its spacious sidings to accommodate all Walsall's local stock, along with sets of excursion stock. The old back yard carriage sidings were retained to stable the two-coach push and pull motor units that worked the Dudley areas and rush-hour specials. After the Dudley services went diesel, when Ryecroft shed closed for steam traction in the spring of 1957, the back yard carriage sidings became used for surplus wagon storage. In 1965, with electrification taking place in Walsall station, all tracks in the back yard sidings were lifted and the site became a car park until the new Saddlers Centre shopping precinct was started in February 1978.

The restaurant

A restaurant was provided when Walsall station was extended by the LNWR in November 1883. The restaurant, which included a buffet and bar, was situated between platforms 2 and 3. It was a long, rectangular, wooden construction of typical LNWR design. This standardisation was brought about by the chief mechanical engineer of the time, Francis William Webb.

At the LNWR headquarters at Crewe, there was a department for restaurant equipment and training facilities for the managers and staff who had to work them. In the case of Walsall station, resident staff were always available for duty, from before the departure of the first morning train for Dudley at 5.55 a.m., until the last arrival from Birmingham to Rugeley at 11.35 p.m. (These times are taken from a Bradshaw timetable for April 1910, but times varied by a few minutes each way until just after the Second World War and nationalisation of the railways.)

The restaurant staff was all female, comprising a manageress, two cooks and on average a dozen waitresses and cleaners. All station catering staff resided in a dormitory upstairs in the old South Staffordshire Railway building in Station Street. It was a long, rectangular room measuring about thirty feet by twelve feet, divided into small bunks for the girls' privacy. The manageress occupied a small, adjoining room of her own.

Discipline was very strict, with great store being set by cleanliness and neat appearance. A two-shift system was in operation for six working days. On Sunday only a buffet remained open for tea and sandwiches. On the two market days, Tuesday and Saturday, more passengers arrived in Walsall and the catering had to be doubled.

The restaurant gained in popularity and became one of the town's most highly regarded dining rooms by the turn of the century. It remained popular until after the First World War. During this time, it was the equal of Walsall's well-known dining rooms 'Dances' in Digbeth and 'Wrights' in nearby Park Street. Prior to the First World War, many prominent local businessmen used the restaurant, many of them from Streetly and Aldridge. They were said to spend their mornings at their desks, then board the Midland Railway train to Walsall to have lunch at the station restaurant, then visit their respective factories for the afternoon administration.

Many travellers visited Walsall to sell their firms' merchandise and were regular clients of the restaurant. Many transactions took place with local businessmen over a well-cooked meal. Many famous music hall artistes were also known to drink in the station's restaurant. However, for the railwaymen on duty in Walsall station, drivers, firemen, guards, signalmen and porters, the restaurant was strictly out of bounds. During the war, the railwaymen were working most abnormal hours and this rule was gradually relaxed. After the nationalisation of railways in 1948, one would find railwaymen in their overalls, sitting down to tea and sandwiches in the restaurant.

When British Rail took over, economies began to take place. In the post-war era, bus travel began to have its effect on travelling habits and working men were able to afford their own motorcars. During the 1950s, many snack bars and cafés started up in business in the town and Walsall station restaurant stopped cooking meals, selling only tea and sandwiches. The restaurant closed down on 16 January 1965, when Dr Beeching withdrew all local railway services. Only the Walsall to Birmingham local service remained, and the few commuters who used this did not require a restaurant. Walsall's once-efficient restaurant disappeared for good and today many citizens are unaware that it ever existed.

Market days

The heyday of travel from Walsall station was during the time that the Midland Railway connected with the well-established LNWR from 1879 until just after the First World War. Weekdays always found the station a hub of activity, especially Tuesday and Saturday, market days in Walsall. Many market traders would be on the first early-morning trains arriving. The trains on market days always had extra vans attached, to cope with the traders' wares. Large wicker baskets were the order of the day then, for moving traders' goods. On other days, the traders would unload at other local markets. With the aid of handcarts and horse-drawn carts for heavy goods, the traders lost no time in getting to the market.

The rush of factory workers and early market shoppers filled the trains, with many standing despite extra carriages being attached to all local trains. This was always a problem for the Walsall stationmaster, who made the decision regarding allocation of extra

Walsall to Dudley push and pull two-coach locomotive passenger train, 1952. The train is on platform 5 of Walsall station. The fast lines were between platforms 3 and 4 with the 'town' side of platform 4 having the 'up fast loop' running beside it, providing platform No. 5. (Reproduced by courtesy of the National Railway Museum, York.)

coaches according to the number of passengers. This was no easy job, taking into account a 'local' starting from Rugeley, picking up at five stations, with Cannock and Hednesford contributing many passengers, and changes in weather making a difference to numbers.

By lunchtime, most market travellers had arrived for their Walsall visit, which might also include a visit to the theatre. During the afternoon and teatime the station was working a normal routine, rush hour and early evening being somewhat calm. From about 9.00 p.m. onwards the station came to life. With the close of business at the market, the time approached for the closure of the theatres and public houses and people would throng to the station for the train home. On platform 2 the bar and restaurant would be filled to capacity with revellers and platforms 1 and 5 would have their buffets full, with standing room only. By about 11.00 p.m., all platforms would be packed with passengers, mainly drunk or merry. Traders, returning with their empty wicker baskets, would find difficulty in moving amongst the throngs of people. Live poultry would be adding to the general hubbub, along with noisy or fretful children, clutching their parents. The engine drivers, approaching the station, would view with trepidation the dense crowds standing inches from the edge of the platform. The non-corridor six-wheel LNWR coaches of that period would be, within seconds, full to capacity, with more standing than sitting. Between 11.00 and 11.30 p.m., many trains for Wolverhampton via North Walsall, Rugeley, Lichfield and Aldridge left Ryecroft Junction. Also trains for Birmingham, Dudley and Wolverhampton leaving via Pleck carried thousands of passengers away from the market, every small station along these lines having its regular passengers who, in those days, made each market day trip to Walsall a happy occasion with something of a party atmosphere. People laughed and enjoyed the trip, a contrast to some of today's morose, straight-faced passengers and the so-called football 'fans'.

Just after midnight, the station became empty. Underneath the gas lights the few night porters would be found busy sweeping-up platforms and preparing for the next morning's early workers' trains. During this tidying-up period, the station would be passed through by approximately one hundred mineral and freight trains taking advantage of the passenger lull. The following days would be busy again on Walsall station but none comparable with market days.

The cab rank

Passengers arriving at Walsall station had only two modes of transport to their residence before the advent of motor transport, the hansom cab and the landau. Whilst the tramcar was the domain of the working class, the middle classes could afford the luxury of the cab. The traveller's requirements were looked after by a highly organized service. At peak times along the length of Station Street, from the old South Staffordshire Railway's buildings to Park Street on the railway side, at least twenty hansom cabs and landaus would be drawn up in line. Most likely, their destinations from Walsall station would be Birmingham Road, Sutton Road, Mellish Road or Lichfield Street, these districts being mainly middle-class areas. Senior citizens state that it was most rare to see one in Ryecroft or Green Lane.

The porters at Walsall station were a very efficient, obliging set of men, who, after the arrival of a train, would work like slaves transferring luggage from train to cab. Obviously it was the tips that made this effort worthwhile, for, in those days at the turn of the century, a three-penny piece or sixpence was a great help to a porter's pay. The cabmen and porters thus formed a very close alliance concerning the tipping habits of the local gentry. Cabs would be 'on duty' from about 5.00 a.m. until midnight to deal with some 160 local departures and arrivals, plus some ten unadvertised workers' specials. This was enough to keep this fleet of cabs and drivers in a state of reasonable employment.

These station cabmen did have the luxury of a small, round, wooden cabin, for messing and clothes drying, opposite the Queen's Hotel near Little Station Street. Around here was a congestion of horse traffic, including many railway horse and dray movements to the parcels office in the old South Staffordshire Railway building. The smell of horse manure was always in evidence in this Station Street area. Today we have the synthetic smell of bus fuel fumes.

To end the memories of the station cab rank, it must have been quite an event to arrive on platform 1, late at night on a 'local' from Birmingham, probably hauled by one of the LNWR Webb 2-4-2 four-feet six-inch tank engines, call a porter for your suitcases and walk out of the old, dim, gas-lit passage into Station Street, giving your ticket to the collector in his small office in the passage. Then you would board your cab after tipping the porter. Sometimes the porter would be seen from the cab, buying, with his tip, hot roasted potatoes from the potato roaster's handcart, always stationed outside the Grand Theatre. The cab would probably turn down Park Street, over The Bridge, where smoke and steam from the trains would be rising, and on past the clattering tramcars and other cabs, eventually to return to the rear of the cab rank. Always, during a working week, Station Street was busy with station work. Today things have changed, with the hapless pedestrian negotiating the hazards of the 'precinct' in order to catch a malodorous, noisy, diesel omnibus.

The Station Street cattle dock

This cattle dock was situated to the rear of platform 1 of Walsall station, which served trains on the down line. Originally the space was limited when the large three-storey Georgian house with its garden was standing at the corner of Station Street and Bridgeman Street, adjacent to the subway. This house was demolished just after the First World War, so more cattle pens were then erected on the extended site.

Midland Goods Yard, c. 1918-1920. The yard was near Walsall station. Bob Barnaby of Essex Street is shown second from the right. The railway used horses in a variety of ways. Horse-drawn parcel drays were used to collect and deliver parcels. Horse power was used to shunt cattle wagons using a number of carefully placed capstans.

Access to the cattle dock was via the down goods loop line that ran into the grain shed adjacent to platform 1. A small turntable was situated on this down goods loop at the entrance to the grain shed. Four roads radiated from this turntable long enough to accommodate six cattle wagons. All the shunting of these cattle wagons was by horsepower via a number of carefully placed capstans. One of the horses that had spent most of its life on the daily dray jobs from Long Street goods deck, and was about to be retired, qualified for this task. A resident shunter was allocated to look after the line of stables running alongside Station Street at this point. It was usual that one of the retired dray drivers or yard shunters had this job after retirement.

During the 1920s, one ex-railwayman looked after the horses until he was almost ninety years old. The stables and yard perimeter were always kept spotlessly clean. He always appeared to be at work and was known to spend all night in the stable with a sick horse, sleeping on straw with the animal.

For the movement of cattle, a well-organised system was in force. Cattle for Pleck, Palfrey, Caldmore and Chuckery arrived via the Midland Railway cattle dock in Tasker Street. From Station Street cattle arrived for Walsall town centre, Birchills, Stafford Street, Butts and Leamore. There was no abattoir in those days for killing cattle, so it was usual for each butcher to slaughter animals on his own premises.

In the case of cows and sheep, special days were allotted for their delivery to Station Street. When unloaded they would be rounded up into a special pen to await the services of a drover. Each animal would be marked to its owner after being bought at a sale some days earlier. When checked with the railway inspector for safe arrival, the drover had the task of shepherding the animals through the streets of Walsall, delivering to butchers' shops en route. As road transport in the shape of motor cars was almost non-existent, his task was fairly easy. However, he did have problems with passing tramcars and the occasional steam lorry. In the case of pigs, it was a problem for them to walk long distances, so local hauliers would collect them in a horse and trap. The cattle dock also had a regular visit of horse vans.

Local haulage contractors and the Birmingham Canal Navigation Company, which was railway owned, used the railway for movement of horses. With the arrival of a passenger train with a horse box attached, the Bridgeman Place shunt engine would immediately shunt the horse box into the down loop for the horse shunter to deal with. Likewise, the same system applied for attaching horse boxes to passenger trains.

The Station Street stables also gave accommodation to canal horses overnight after they had worked boats to the many wharfs situated along the Walsall arm. The system of cattle movements was in operation until just before the Second World War. About 1937, a new abattoir was opened in Short Acre Street and, with the more economical method of moving cattle by road transport, animals began to be moved direct from farm to Short Acre Street abattoir. In any case the expanding volume of traffic was creating a hazard when moving cattle from Station Street, along Stafford Street, to Short Acre, but the Second World War gave the Station Street cattle dock a new lease of life.

From the end of the war to about 1950, all cattle movements declined rapidly and, by 1954, all operations ceased, leaving the yard to fall into a state of decay. About 1958, the cattle pens and stables were demolished and the land was used for a car park, reserved solely for the use of British Rail staff.

Walsall railway station parcels office

The parcels office situated in the old South Staffordshire Railway building in Station Street was, from the turn of the century until after the Second World War, a constant hive of activity. From 6.00 a.m. until midnight a constant battle was in progress to despatch and receive parcels. The office interior was always gloomy, containing only a small number of gas lamps to illuminate parcels stacked almost up to the roof (approximately ten feet). There was just about enough room to manoeuvre the two-wheeled handcarts so essential to a railway station. The atmosphere was typical of the LNWR. The high clerks' desks with hinged lid and the tall, strong chairs were always in use. Until the 1930s quill pens were used in the red and black inkpots and invoices and paperwork were to be seen in neat, tidy piles on every available desk space. In a separate office, within the main parcels department, was the parcel chief supervisor, who had the task of organising this efficient service.

To avoid confusion, the parcels office was divided into two sections, one for in-going parcels and the other for out-going. The main bulk of parcels to and from the office came through a raised doorway of some eight feet by six feet. Throughout the day a covered horse-drawn dray would occupy the space adjacent to this doorway. It is hard, in view of our way of life today, to imagine the activity that took place outside the Station Street parcels office. At times, as many as six covered drays would be waiting their turn to unload and load. The railway had, on average, six horse-drawn parcel drays in LNWR and early LMS days. Almost all large Walsall factories owned their own private drays. Once a day these would pay at least one visit to Walsall parcels office. This was particularly the case with Walsall's leather factories. In the office the smell of leather was distinctive amidst the various other parcels and on a summer's day the smell of horse manure was a thing one had to get used to. From Station Street, the parcels office cobblestone apron dipped down to the footpath. When departing with a full load, the poor horses sometimes had problems, usually solved by raised voices from the draymen and a crack of the whip.

Next to the main delivery door was a small doorway leading into a little room about the size of a small garden shed. This was for small private parcels. It was well patronised and people sometimes had to wait their turn to be served.

The staff usually worked shifts starting before the first passenger train departure, the 5.55 a.m. Walsall to Dudley, and until after the arrival of the last passengers into Walsall station from Wolverhampton at 11.47 p.m. The senior parcels clerk and assistants worked morning and late turns. The rest of the staff worked various split turns subject to traffic requirements. A split turn remembered by Mr Cyril Smith during the 1920s was 6.30 a.m. to 11.00 a.m., then returning at 4.30 p.m. until 11.30 p.m. The parcel clerks also had to learn the booking office system so that, at times of heavy traffic, clerks would transfer offices, allowing flexible operation of both parcels and passenger operations.

During a working day some ninety passenger trains arrived and departed at Walsall's platforms. In most cases the guards' vans would be full to capacity. It has been known for a guard's van to be so full that the guard had to ride in the nearest passenger compartment. Over the covered footbridge a constant stream of parcels moved between platforms and parcels office. The parcels office system was severely taxed during the few weeks prior to Christmas. Most of the staff worked twelve-hour shifts, the overtime being most welcome. To help out, staff from other local railway departments would work four hours' special duty, moving parcels, after their normal eight-hour shift. On platform 1 to the rear of the parcels office the congestion of Christmas parcels sometimes left very little space for passengers. On the platforms during this Christmas rush there was always a member of the railway police. This was not surprising, considering that it was common practice for people to send turkeys via passenger parcels with only a card tied with string around the turkey's neck. Problems occurred with the arrival of each passenger train. With only a few minutes' stopping time, unloading and loading the goods compartment required some effort from the porters and parcel staff. The guard, in the meantime, had to attend to the passengers. The festive season also brought the problem of vast numbers of Christmas trees. These were a nuisance for storing and handling. Situated on the down side of Walsall station were two bays sufficient to accommodate three large vans or coaches. The down line bay was known as the Cannock Bay and the up line bay the Sutton Bay. These bays were worked to capacity with parcels traffic for most of the year. For the Christmas period night work, using the slow lines platforms 1 and 2 after the passenger trains stopped running, would relieve the congestion.

In pre-Second World War days most of the leather factories in Walsall would deposit their parcels daily. It was at teatime that the rush began. Shannons, clothiers of George Street, sent a regular deposit of 700 parcels. With leather factories depositing parcels as well, the work for the parcels clerks was staggering, considering that every parcel had to be recorded and stamped. By about 8.00 p.m. at least 2,000 parcels would have been handled. By late evening they would all have left on the various evening local passenger trains.

Some of the parcels office consignments were very sad. The bodies of local people living away from Walsall or of visitors to Walsall all had to be moved by passenger train

Walsall No. 2 signal box, 1958. The signal box was on the up side tracks, Pleck side of Bridgeman Street subway. The signalman shown was a Cannock councillor.

before the days of efficient road transport. All coffins would be moved from horse-drawn hearses to guards vans directly, so as not to be left in either the parcels office or on the platform.

Local fishmongers had regular deliveries of supplies, but these were always collected direct from the trains. Only the paperwork concerned the parcels clerks.

Walsall parcels office, like all ex-LNWR and later LMS offices, provided a service for conveying luggage to hotels or digs. The same system worked on your return. Prior to the Second World War, the average price according to distance was between two shillings and sixpence and five shillings. This service according to geography was shared with other railway companies. It was very rare for luggage to be mislaid and if it was the company accepted liability and paid compensation.

Perhaps the most unusual consignment that was dispatched from the parcels office was a regular order of white mice and rats for medical research. Cartons of these animals were delivered by express passenger parcels to various doctors and specialists in Harley Street, London, for use in experiments. A box of these mice and rats would cost about two shillings, including delivery to Harley Street.

Sunday was sometimes a busy day for the parcels clerks when theatrical groups arrived in town complete with costumes and props. Considering each theatre had about a dozen turns, a lot of work was involved. In the case of a travelling revue, special coaches would be added to a local passenger train. All the company's costumes and props had to be unloaded and booked. Station porters and parcels staff sometimes used the large station trolleys to manhandle the artistes' goods directly to the Grand and Her Majesty's Theatres. It was lucrative work, with an abundance of tips. Sometimes a porter would be five shillings better off with visits from 'the theatricals'. In the 1900 to 1930 period this was big money.

The parcels office was, therefore, always a very important means of moving goods until just after the Second World War. By then an institution was about to come to an end. Between the years 1950 to 1960 a rival, in the shape of road haulage parcel carriers, began to usurp the place of the time-honoured system of rail parcels delivery. Speed and door-to-door delivery plus cheap rates made it more economical for the customer. Also, during the late 1960s the lucrative pigeon traffic was lost as flying clubs began buying their own pigeon transporters. The parcels office trade had dwindled to a very low trickle by the time the old Station Street buildings were demolished in 1979. The staff comprised only one leading railway clerk. Today's new parcels office is situated in the same place as its predecessor and it is shaped like a modern bungalow. Nothing of character remains to compare with the old South Staffordshire Railway building in Station Street.

Walsall station, 1918

The late Jack Reynolds, engine driver, of Ryecroft shed, 1908 to 1958, witnessed a happy event. This took place on Walsall station just after the end of the First World War. It was the return of the local battalion of the 5th South Staffordshire Regiment. The regimental band stood on platform 1 in full regalia. All platforms were full to capacity with soldiers' families and loved ones. In addition, large crowds gathered in Park Street, The Bridge and Lichfield Street as far as Whittimere Street Drill Hall. Almost the entire population of Walsall found time for this event, including vast numbers of flag-waving children. The special troop train arrived in Walsall via Ryecroft Junction down the St Paul cutting. As the train passed under Littleton Street Bridge, railway fog detonators, placed some three feet apart from the station confines, were exploded. On arrival, the soldiers formed ranks behind the band and departed to the drill hall to disband.

With regard to the many fog signals placed on the line, it must be assumed that the LNWR local management, along with the Walsall stationmaster, had planned this affair and informed the driver to proceed, breaking all instructions in the strict railway safety rule book. For once all railway staff in LNWR employment ignored the rulebook and safety procedures of which this railway was proud, but it is not often that a world war ends.

Walsall station 1920-1964: pigeon traffic

Over the years Walsall station, during the appropriate pigeon-flying season, dealt with vast numbers of pigeon specials to most parts of the United Kingdom, with a number of birds destined to the Continent. Usually Friday evenings saw the most activity for the parcels department staff and porters. Each basket of pigeons was individually booked and costed by the parcels office staff. On Friday evenings a special train consisting of approximately ten carriage-size parcel vans would be made up on platform 1. All day long local pigeon fanciers would deposit their baskets of birds at their local station to be conveyed to Walsall station on local passenger trains. These pick-up stations were along the Rugeley to Walsall, Lichfield to Walsall, Sutton to Walsall, and Dudley to Walsall lines. Also towards teatime many local fanciers could be seen in Station Street depositing their baskets of birds which had been carried on wheelbarrows or on a bicycle fitted with a rear wheel platform carrier. The pigeon baskets would be held on by used inner cycle tubes. Prior to the arrival of the special train, platform 1 would be almost full to capacity with no room for potential passengers.

The pigeon special ran between local passenger trains and for transit movements all railway pigeon specials ran as a normal parcels train code. A Friday night pigeon special well remembered by Ryecroft shed men was the direct train to Bath. Its destination was Templecombe, a favourite place to release birds. Another destination was Weymouth, but local Ryecroft men only knew the road to Bath and some were relieved at Gloucester. Many of the Weymouth birds were for transit to the Continent.

All these long-distance pigeon trains from Walsall were organised by local pigeon clubs who supplied conveyors to accompany the birds and attend to feeding, etc. Finance was arranged between the clubs and the railway. A problem occurred from 1957 when all local train services changed over to the new local diesel multiple units. When a Friday night pigeon special was made up in Walsall station, all the local passenger trains would add extra vans to their stock to accommodate the extra load. When one or two vans were attached to the new DMU trains their power was insufficient to deal with the loads, especially on the Rugeley to Hednesford gradient. Thus until 1964 a special steam-hauled van train ran on local lines in between local passenger trains to deal with the problem. After steam traction ceased in this area, a diesel loco took over. This did not last for long however as road transport took over all local pigeon movements. Amongst local pigeon fanciers there is a theory that road haulage of pigeons does not give the birds a comfortable ride due to hard bouncing and frequent stopping and starting of lorries and the motorway fumes. This is in contrast to a smooth railway ride which used to enable the birds to arrive at their destination in a relaxed and restful condition. With the present-day administration of British railways, it is not likely that mass pigeon transit will ever take place again by rail.

The ghost train

This was the name given to a special goods train working through Walsall station during the 1930s. The train concerned was a special out-of-gauge load running from Washwood Heath sidings, Birmingham, to Birkenhead docks on Merseyside. During the days of the Indian Empire various maharajas owned their own personal luxurious railway coaches. These private railway coaches were manufactured at Metro-Cammel coachworks, Washwood Heath, Birmingham. These coaches were the last thing in splendour of design and included gold-plated bathroom and toilet facilities. Because they were built to a larger size than the standard British Railway carriage, problems occurred if they had to be moved on our limited-gauge railway system. For conveyance of non-standard railway loads, the railway companies built special low-load bogie wagons with the centre bottom only just above rail level. Also side hand-screw jacks enabled a load to be moved sideways to avoid bridge or tunnel obstructions. These special wagons were used on the special working through Walsall station. The special out-of-gauge load left Washwood Heath on late Saturday evening after the last passenger local trains ran. It was routed over the old Midland line via Walsall then onto the Grand Junction line to Bushbury Junction and Stafford, then diverting to the GWR system at Shrewsbury. From there it went to Birkenhead docks, arriving in the early hours of Monday morning. It appears that Walsall station was the major problem on this route. The main culprit was Park Street tunnel with its restricted clearances.

Walsall station regulations allowed permissive working within the station limits controlled by Walsall signal boxes 2 and 3. The regulations allowed locomotives to work the wrong line for attaching and detaching coaches on vans to local passenger trains. This wrong line movement procedure was always referred to by railwaymen as Bang Road because of what would happen should signalling rules be ignored. Very strict rules applied to this practice and accidents were unknown in Walsall station.

To assist in these movements, many small 'call on' or 'dwarf' signals were positioned facing the up and down sides of Walsall station, including a number under the confines of Park Street tunnel. To enable the special out-of-gauge load to pass under Park Street, it was deemed necessary to remove some of these 'call on' signals from their bases to relieve obstruction to the passing special and also to save time. To deal with this situation the Walsall permanent way engineer at the New Mills depot would receive orders to dismantle these signals at the appropriate time. This meant much welcome overtime for the local permanent way men. After the first out-of-gauge load movement was successfully finalised, a plan was established for future movements of these special maharajas' personal coaches.

It is many years now and part of history since these transfers took place, but one memory remains of the era in Walsall station, among local railwaymen of the permanent way staff and others, relating to a certain permanent way worker involved in the dismantling and installing of the Walsall station 'call on' or 'dwarf' signals whose name was Thomas Dodd. This Mr Thomas Dodd was a very loyal, efficient track worker and was between four and five feet in height. Subsequently his colleagues somehow began to refer to all these 'dwarf' call on signals as 'Tommy Dodds' after this permanent way worker. Even today in this modern electric railway age, when all these mechanical 'call on' or 'dwarf' signals have been replaced by small coloured-light ground signals in shunt movements, they are still referred to within the vicinity of Walsall as 'Tommy Dodds'.

The Pines Express in Walsall station

Walsall station has always been essentially a local passenger station. Since the first station, situated in Bridgeman Place, opened in 1847, passengers from Walsall have had to travel to Birmingham for a main line express train. After the Railway Grouping Act of 1923, which formed the London Midland and Scottish Railway, Walsall station was handling up to 1,000 train movements per twenty-four hours, these being mostly mineral and goods trains and light engine movements, but from 5.55 a.m. until 11.45 p.m. some 120 local passenger trains served Walsall. Also a number of excursions either started from or picked up in Walsall station, but in the summer of 1927 Walsall station dealt for the one and only time with an express, although only on Saturdays during the summer. It was the new Pines Express running between Manchester and Bournemouth, so named after the pine forests of Hampshire which the express passed through. The weekday Pines Express passed just inside the Walsall boundary on the down journey, along the old Grand Junction line at Bescot, but in the up direction it ran along the Stour Valley line between Wolverhampton and Birmingham. However on each summer Saturday the Pines Express was diverted via Walsall.

Although the Pines Express was diverted from Darlaston Junction into Walsall station then over the Midland line to Water Orton and via Camp Hill, avoiding the line to the

Walsall station, 1958. The trains shown are the Pines Express on platform 1 about to depart for Bournemouth with locomotive 45662 and parcels train on middle road with locomotive 45631 which will run light engine via the Cannock line to Crewe.

south, it was not booked in the Bradshaw timetable to pick up passengers in Walsall. Any Bournemouth passengers from Walsall and Birmingham had their own summer special train during the morning. The original Pines Express during summer Saturdays was invariably full to capacity after leaving Crewe. The Pines Express did, however, change engines on arrival in Walsall station in both up and down directions. As the summer service progressed to the August Bank Holiday relief 'Pines' followed the main 'Pines' train. The up arrival in Walsall was at about midday, with reliefs following about thirty minutes behind. Local railwaymen are of the opinion that only two relief 'Pines' were permitted after the main 'Pines'. This was so as not to overload the difficult margins that were working to capacity over the Bath to Bournemouth section of the Somerset & Dorset Railway. The engines of the Pines were serviced at Ryecroft shed until 1956 when Bescot shed took over Ryecroft's steam links so that Ryecroft could be used for the new diesel multiple units which phased out local steam passenger trains.

The Pines' engines and crew came from Longsight shed in Manchester. The guard booked off at Walsall station and took up his duty again when the Pines engine left

Ryecroft shed about 2.30 p.m. to work the down 'Pines' back to Manchester at approximately 3.15 p.m. With the arrival on Walsall's No. 1 platform of the up Pines, the engine lost no time uncoupling to run light engine (i.e. without rolling stock) to Ryecroft shed. In platform 1A, known as the Cannock Bay, was the engine or reliefs to take the Pines Express on the next stage to Bath. These engines and crew were from Saltley shed in Birmingham, running light engines to Walsall. The signalmen in Walsall No. 3 signal box and No. 2 signal box had to work to fine margins for the change of engines. No. 3 box had the most difficult manoeuvres to attend to. It is believed that ten minutes were allowed for this change. During this time station staff were responsible for topping up the water tank of the restaurant car. With this change of engines in Walsall station, friction was always in evidence between Ryecroft men of the North Western division and the Saltley men from the Midland Division of the LMS Railway. Ryecroft men objected to Saltley men working the Pines from their territory. In pre-war days railwaymen were always insisting on their rights for extra work to obtain extra money to supplement their not-too-well-paid jobs during the Depression. Nevertheless, they did fare better financially than some other workers.

During the 1930s Walsall station and local viewing spots were, on summer Saturdays, an attraction for many trainspotters. One gentleman still recalls the many named engines that arrived from Manchester. The down Pines Express would arrive in Walsall at approximately 12.00 p.m. The engine change took place with the usual efficiency. This time the main work was under the jurisdiction of Walsall No. 2 signal box. The Pines was invariably double-headed. The light engines then had to return to Saltley shed but one feature that was interesting to local trainspotters was that, upon reaching Ryecroft Junction, Ryecroft signal box turned them up the Walsall to Wolverhampton Midland line to North Walsall Junction. Here they crossed over tracks in the old North Walsall station to run chimney-first to Lichfield Road Junction, then on to Saltley shed. This was the moment of glory for North Walsall signal box as throughout its existence nothing more than passenger tank engines or Midland class 2 and 3 tender engines ever used this line. From 1936 Stanier class 5 and Fowler Crabs, with the occasional new 5XP Jubilee, were regular performers, coupled to either a Standard Compound or Midland class 2. The most splendid sight in my railway memories was of the visit to North Walsall Junction of a brand new Jubilee No. 5557 *New Brunswick* coupled to a crimson Midland Compound after working the Pines Express.

Walsall railway station: the travellers

A now forgotten feature of Walsall station life was the ever-constant visits of the travellers. These travellers, the predecessors of the present-day 'reps', included travelling sales representatives and firms' executives. Nowadays they use a company car or their own vehicles.

Before the Second World War and back to mid-Victorian times, all communication for industrial and shopping transactions was performed by travellers who, for six days a week, when not engaged in interviews regarding purchasing or selling goods, spent most of their life in railway compartments or hotels. With Walsall being very famous for its leather products, a constant flow of leather salesmen passed through Walsall station. Also in evidence were many travellers representing cotton mills in Lancashire. The two busy days for arrival of travellers were Tuesdays and Wednesdays. A hundred or more of these travellers would arrive on those days complete with their samples. A number of heavy suitcases would be the normal travelling gear, but some firms provided their travellers with large wicker baskets with skids underneath for sliding along platforms. Sometimes these baskets, along with other goods, filled the guard's van to capacity, resulting in the guard having to travel in one of the adjacent coaches.

Eagerly awaiting the travellers on the station were two official outside porters. Under LNWR rules, most large stations were allocated a number of outside porters, identified by an armband issued by the company. They were not paid by the company, but had the freedom of the station to meet trains and deliver goods, parcels etc. to various local firms and shops working on a commission basis. The outside porters had their regular clients who knew their routine. The porters gave a reliable service and had a good financial reward.

The majority of travellers with light samples would carry their own suitcases and join the Station Street cab rank for transport to local factories and stores. When these travellers arrived out of the two station entrances, the barrow boys always confronted them. These barrow boys, with hand-made wheel carts, were envious of the outside porters. The barrow boys were not allowed on the platforms. Some of them were, indeed, characters like the notorious Irishmen who regularly met the travellers who had to visit some fifty or more town shops on their regular visits. Evidently, for most of the day they wheeled their barrows from shop to shop, returning to the station about teatime. A day's wage was approximately three and six for a day's hard slog. After being paid, most of these barrow boys would retire to one of the small backstreet public houses, leaving their barrows outside. By turning-out time they would be in a high state of intoxication and many elder citizens of Walsall recall seeing these barrow boys being wheeled home at night, dead drunk, on their own barrows.

A number of travellers representing the textile mills of Lancashire were prominent in Walsall. These travellers, noted for their smart appearance, plied their clothing and cotton samples around Walsall and district for most of the day and by teatime they would besiege the telegraph office on platform 1 to inform their respective mills who immediately responded to a request for a delivery. The local telegraph clerks could claim to know of every cotton mill in Lancashire. It was not until the mid-1920s that telephones were installed to help the congestion at Walsall station's telegraph office.

The numbers of these old time travellers through Walsall station began to decline rapidly in about 1930. Most firms took advantage of the reliability of the motorcar and by the Second World War travellers at Walsall station gradually disappeared from the scene.

The prisoners

A daily sight at Walsall station was the arrival and departure of the 'Black Maria', from Walsall's Goodall Street police station. All prisoners awaiting trial, or conviction by a local court, had to be transferred by railway to Winson Green Prison, Birmingham. Having a station at Winson Green made the movement of prisoners between Walsall police station and gaol relatively easy. The method for moving prisoners was for the police to request Walsall's stationmaster to reserve special compartments on a Walsall to Birmingham local train, running via Soho loop.

Working to a strict timetable, a horse-drawn Black Maria would leave Goodall Street police station to journey down High Street with its inmates handcuffed to burly policemen inside, with others alongside the driver on top. Turning left at The Bridge, it ran via Bradford Street and under the subway, turning into Station Street. On arrival, railway police would be waiting to escort civilian police and prisoners to the train. The same procedure took place on the return trip.

Situated between platforms 4 and 5 was the railway police and detective office. The transfer of prisoners was only a small part of their duty. They had the task of escorting criminals from all regions of England to be handed over to the civilian police. These Walsall station railway police were also responsible for policing the railway well outside the Walsall Borough boundary. In addition, they were responsible for patrolling the local railway-owned canal system.

At some time about the early 1930s, police began to take advantage of the motorcar for transport of prisoners. Thus, the sight of handcuffed criminals on Walsall station ended.

Milk

Until about 1930, Walsall milk supplies were brought in by railway. As the railway system in the Walsall area reached the peak of its operations in about 1879, a system evolved gradually whereby farmers could easily despatch milk from farm to town.

From the late Victorian era until the end of the First World War, the milk traffic on Walsall station was a regular daily event. During the arrival of the first morning passenger trains, large numbers of labelled seventeen-gallon milk churns would be deposited from guards' vans. A simple but effective routine commenced. At certain country railway stations, a farmer with pony and trap would deposit a number of milk churns destined for certain Walsall dairymen. These were placed on the platform near to where the guard's van would stop in the early morning hours. Empty churns returned during the previous day would be taken back to the farm.

From 6.00 a.m. onwards, a number of local dairymen with horses and drays would stand in Station Street ready for their day's business. Considerable activity and milk transactions would take place on the surrounding footpaths of the station premises. With trains arriving on five platforms at regular intervals until 9.30 a.m., rows of milk churns were left standing like soldiers on parade after the departure of the trains.

Before the arrival of a train, the respective platform would be thronged with passengers. Within minutes the passengers would disappear onto the train, leaving a few porters with parcels and milk churns. Milkmen to move the full churns to the Station Street entrance would then join the porters. Moving these full churns was indeed a remarkable sight. Most milkmen and porters became very skilled in the art of spinning a churn at considerable speed along the various platforms and over the wooden crossing boards situated on the up side of the station. The churns were eventually spun out of the Station Street entrance.

Amongst the horse-drawn cabs and parcel vans, one would find a number of the horse-drawn two-wheel milk traps. Many famous Walsall dairymen would be there. The principal firms around the time of the First World War would be H.P. Woolner of Eastbourne Street, Goulden Brothers Ltd of Lichfield Street, Warner's Dairy of Warwick

Street, Field's Dairy of Blue Lane and W.E. Claridge of Lord Street. Smaller representatives of the dairy trade were Mcfarlane & Wakeman, Allen's Dairy and Pym's Dairy. The main dairymen supplied many other small traders from their own premises.

During the loading of the milk churns, numerous milkmen with small handcarts could be seen buying small quantities of milk from the main dealers on a cash basis. These characters would have their own rounds among the working-class terraced houses, selling milk in pint jugs to housewives. By mid-morning the milk activity at the Station Street entrance would cease, leaving parcel vans room to manoeuvre about their own premises.

During the early 1930s, the motor lorry was taking over milk delivery from Walsall station. The dairy owners soon found it more economical to visit farms and collect their own milk direct. By the outbreak of the Second World War, a milk churn on Walsall station was a rare sight.

The Walsall Co-op Society was in the process of building a very efficient milk delivery system and opened a modern dairy in Midland Road on 10 July 1937. From the opening date until about 1950, the LMS Railway still delivered milk to the Co-op. With a rising population, the milk needs for Walsall were beyond the limited means of seventeen-gallon churns. Milk tankers loaded onto railway low-loaders delivered the Co-op milk supply. These wagons shunted to the Walsall Midland sidings. An old cattle ramp siding at the Tasker Street end was used to unload the milk tankers. A railway lorry then towed the milk tanker to the nearby Co-op Milk Dairy to deposit its contents, by gravity, into the low-lying storage tanks. Within about an hour, the empty tanker would be back on its railway wagon to return to its rural destination.

This system finally gave way to direct road transport in about 1950. But for the advent of the Second World War, it would have been axed long before. After the Second World War, the only milk delivered was for the station snack bar cum restaurant and staff offices. This was indeed very different from the days when the whole of Walsall more or less depended on its station for its domestic milk supply.

The hop pickers

Before the advent of motor travel there was a service from Walsall station for hop pickers, during the appropriate season. These local hop pickers were usually made up of small groups of families from the working-class areas of Walsall – mainly from the Ryecroft, Birchills or Green Lane areas. There was never a large-scale exodus of hop pickers like the London cockneys en route for the Kent hop fields. Instead Walsall station had to despatch small groups destined for the Worcester, Cleobury Mortimer and Hereford hop fields. The route was a joint venture between the GWR and LNWR and later LMS systems. All Walsall hop pickers travelled to the hop fields via Dudley. Owing to the small numbers of these people, it was not economically viable to run a special train from Walsall. Instead arrangements were made to attach two coaches to the Saturday morning Walsall to Dudley motor train. At Dudley station these two coaches were attached to a GWR local train working between Wolverhampton and Worcester. The same procedure took place in reverse on the return journey.

Amusing tales are told by local railwaymen about the return of the hop pickers' coaches to Walsall station. The hop pickers spent at least a week or more bedding down on straw in various barns and farm buildings. They also had to live in most unsanitary conditions and would be alive with lice and fleas. This resulted in the local station carriage cleaners having to fumigate the stock before it went back into service. The ticket collectors used to dread these return events and were most thankful that the hop season did not last too long.

Sometimes the hop pickers arrived on Saturday teatime and would leave some of their blankets and clothing bundles in the parcels office while they spent some of their pay in the local pubs. Usually they were there until closing time and their belongings would remain until Monday, much to the discomfort of the parcels clerks.

One amusing tale of the 1920s was of an old man who had a pram containing all his requirements. When he deposited the pram with the parcels clerk he objected to the price of ninepence for storage. 'How much to leave a parcel?' he enquired of the parcels clerk. 'Four pence,' replied the clerk and the old man made his way out of the door. 'Got rid of him,' thought the clerk as he dealt with his paperwork. Twenty minutes later the old man reappeared with a large parcel made from old newspapers and knotted string. Banging fourpence on the desk he picked up his receipt and departed. The clerk decided to investigate the contents of this most unusual and untidy parcel. To his astonishment he found the body of a pram and inside the structure four wheels, two axles and the handlebars. The clerk saw the funny side of this episode and still laughed in 1979, fifty years later, at this character and his mode of life.

The hop pickers began to use road transport in the early 1930s. Motor coaches of old stock were owned by their employers and many hop pickers were transported in the back of motor lorries direct to the hop fields. After the Second World War no direct railway coaches were put on Dudley trains. It is believed a few hop pickers used the normal service trains for a few more years. By 1979 this annual hop picking was almost forgotten in Walsall.

The Walsall station boat

When the South Staffordshire Railway constructed the first railway into Walsall in 1849, the engineers built the line from the northern direction alongside the Ford Brook River, a tributary of the River Tame. From Ryecroft into St Paul's cutting the railway was slightly lower than the river and the lowest point was Park Street underneath which the railway ran. The river also flowed under Walsall Bridge where it was covered in. This tunnel was extended in the late 1880s when the new Town Hall was erected. By the turn of the century the Ford Brook went underground from the St Paul's area to Bradford Place except for a short length at the rear of the Imperial Cinema in Darwall Street. Walsall's first station was enlarged in 1883 when the Midland Railway merged with the LNWR who had acquired the South Staffordshire Railway in 1861. From the onset of the railway in Walsall, a problem arose if there were severe thunderstorms and/or heavy snowfall. When the volume of water exceeded the capacity of the bridge tunnel area, the overspill always ran along the railway tracks to flood Walsall station to well above platform level. It flooded also the Bridgeman Street subway. Walsall station had floods every few years that put the station out of action for a few days and these occurred until 1979 when the Ford Brook was diverted via a twin tunnel from Ryecroft to New Mills, Pleck.

Prior to 1965 all signalling within Walsall station confines was mechanical and after some days under water the signals could, with the aid of oiling point and signal wires, be got going again in a short time. The signal and telegraph departments, as with the permanent way department, gained financially from overtime allotted during the annual flooding. After 1965 British Rail built a power signal box at Pleck Junction with all signals and points electrified. Thus when flooding occurred, the points, electric fittings and cables sustained water damage and had to be replaced at substantial cost.

In 1980 a very heavy snowfall occurred locally, followed by a rapid temperature rise and accompanied by heavy rain fall. The twin tunnel entrance adjacent to Butts Bridge coped with the extra volume of water until flotsam in great quantities and in the shape of timber, used car tyres, plastic bags and weeds blocked the tunnel inlet, resulting once more in Walsall station being flooded, with some thousands of pounds of damage yet again to its signalling system. Also most of the Saddlers Centre, then under construction, suffered damage to motor equipment. After this folly it was seen fit to erect steel gratings to the tunnel entrance and at least up to February 1994 there was no further flooding. During heavy rain and thaws however the public works department were at work clearing the accumulating debris. In these conditions a lorry could quickly be filled with flotsam.

To help deal with Walsall station floods in LNWR days, the company issued a rowing boat to Walsall station for use by the stationmaster to examine the station confines. Many is the time that the signalman in Walsall No. 3 signal box, situated under the concourse, had to be rescued as the water was at times more than six feet deep. The boat was kept at Walsall permanent way depot in Rollingmill Street. At first a horse-drawn goods dray would convey the boat to the station but later one of the new Scammel mechanical horse trucks did the job. Looking back with hindsight, this continual flooding of Walsall station

Above and opposite: *Flood at Walsall station, 13 May 1886. Walsall station was flooded regularly from 1849-1980. Flooding was due to the fact that the line was lower than the Ford Brook which ran under the centre of Walsall. A station boat, shown here, was provided for use at such times.*

must, over a period of some 140 years, have cost the South Staffordshire Railway, LNWR and British Rail a considerable sum of money in lost revenue and repairs, passenger receipts and inconvenience to trade.

I have often wondered whether, if the engineer of the first South Staffordshire line, J.R. McLean, had constructed the line into Walsall station some ten feet higher with the station elevated to the level of Park Street, the disruption of traffic would have been avoided. However, Park Street, one of Walsall's main shopping streets, would have had a different perspective. It might have been carried under the railway by a tunnel but that might have been liable to flooding. However since the last flood, with the new Ford Brook tunnel diversion and its protective ends plus constant public works attendance when the river is in flood, no station floods have occurred.

Other local titles published by The History Press

Buildings of Walsall An Illustrated Architectural History
PETER ARNOLD

This book describes and illustrates some of the most historically important architecture to be seen in Walsall today and will serve as a useful guide for those wishing to explore and learn more about the modern Walsall Metropolitan Borough's history through its buildings. The New Art Gallery has put Walsall on the UK cultural map, but there are still many architectural secrets little recognised even by locals.
0 7524 2498 X

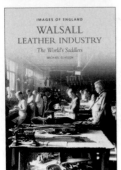

Walsall Football Club
GEOFF ALLMAN

Walsall Football Club's history is full of dedication, whether it be that of the players, the managers, the scouts, the fans who have supported through the dark days, or the directors – some of whom gave virtually all they had to keep the club in existence. The collection of images in this book captures over 100 years of glory days and heartaches and includes those past Walsall players who have gone on to become household names.
0 7524 2091 7

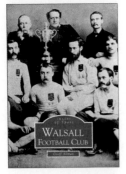

Walsall Leather Industry The World's Saddlers
MICHAEL GLASSON

For nearly 200 years Walsall has been a major centre of the leather industry, exporting saddles, bridles and a variety of horse equipment to most corners of the world. At its peak the industry employed over 10,000 men and women, with the British Army being the single biggest customer. These days Walsall maintains an international reputation for its products, and not surprisingly the town has been called the saddlery 'capital' of the world.
0 7524 2793 8

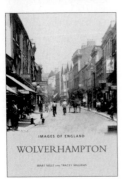

Wolverhampton
MARY MILLS AND TRACEY WILLIAMS

The photographs in this collection recall the changes Wolverhampton underwent between the 1860s and 1960s, a century during which the town centre saw the completion of slum clearance programmes, the building of the ring road, and the construction of two major shopping centres. Each picture brings to life a town our forefathers must have known, and reminds us of a past which has all but vanished.
0 7524 3020 3

If you are interested in purchasing other books published by The History Press, or in case you have difficulty finding any History Press books in your local bookshop, you can also place orders directly through our website
www.thehistorypress.co.uk